Jack London and Hawaii

The Adventures of Charmian and Jack
London in Hawaii

by

Charmian K. London

TROTAMUNDAS PRESS

Trotamundas Press Ltd.
The Meridian, 4 Copthall House, Station Square, Coventry
CV1 2FL, UK

"Jack London and Hawaii" by Charmian K. London

First published in 1918

ISBN: 978-1-906393-08-3

Trotamundas Press is an international publisher specializing in travel literature written by women travellers from different countries and cultures.

Our mission is to bring back into print great travel books written by women around the world which have been forgotten. We publish in several languages.

It is our privilege to rescue those travel stories which were widely acclaimed in the past and that are still relevant nowadays to help us understand better the diversity of the countries and the world.

The travel stories also make an enjoyable reading, full of adventure and the excitement of discovery.

We are proud to help preserving the memory of all those amazing women travellers which were unjustly forgotten and hope that you will enjoy reading about their interesting experiences as much as we have enjoyed researching them.

www.trotamundaspress.com

Charmian Kittredge London
(1871-1955)

"They were an ideal match...Jack and Charmian. She was the comrade for whom Jack had sought. She was fearless and game for any adventure he might dream up and yet always ultrafeminine. She filled his every need and more during their years of marriage"

Russ Kingman

Charmian Kittredge was born in 1871 and following the death of her mother in 1877 she was sent to Oakland to be raised by an aunt. Her father died shortly afterwards due to poor health. She was a solitary girl who enjoyed riding horses, reading books, drawing, playing piano and swimming. Charmian's aunt educated her at home under ideas of feminism, vegetarianism and socialism. However, Charmian did not feel well treated by her aunt and longed to be independent.

Charmian's independent spirit led her to support herself by working as a secretary for a shipping company in San Francisco, something unusual for a middle class girl at the time. She had attended Mills Academy and paid for her college tuition by working as a secretary to the founder, Susan Mills. For women to graduate from High School, let alone from a university education, was highly unusual at the time.

Charmian was an accomplished horse rider and a published photographer as well. She took pride in being able to afford her own horse, its stabling and a part-time Swedish maid. During the 1890's Charmian wrote reviews and articles for "Overland Monthly" in her spare time. She first met Jack London during one of his visits to the editors and they became casual friends. At the time Charmian was involved with another man and was not attracted to Jack London. Jack was married to Bess Maddern. However, in the summer of 1904 and following a series of coincidental meetings, they fell in love. Jack divorced and a year later they married and went to live in Glen Ellen Farm.
Charmian became Jack's secretary and in exchange he gave her his unpublished manuscripts.

Jack and Charmian sailed across the South Pacific in 1907-09 in the "Snark". It was going to be a seven year trip but it was cut short due to a skin infection contracted by Jack during the trip. Following this journey, Charmian wrote two books "The Log of the Snark" and "Our Hawaii". During the final two years of Jack London's life, under Charmian's persuassion, they lived for long periods in Hawaii. Jack admired Charmian's artistic talents in music and drawing and her ability to combine her unique mixture of feminine style with unconventionality. He found her a comrade, both strong and tender, and dedicated many loving notes to her, like the following in "Little Lady of the Big House": "The years pass. You and I pass. But yet our love abides – more firmly, more deeply, more surely, for we have built our love for each other, not for the sand, but upon the rock".

Despite his heavy drinking and her bouts of depression, they helped and nurtured each other through life's tragedies, like the loss of a daughter at birth, the miscarriage of another child, the fire at Wolf House - Jack's dream house - which destroyed the house as soon as it reached completion , and Jack's failing health.

Charmian presuaded Jack to spend time in Hawaii in 1915 and again in 1916, where he seemed better able to relax and more willing to take care of himself. On November 22, 1916, Jack London died of gatrointestinal uremic poisoning. He was 40 years old.

Following his death, Charmian tried to save Beauty Ranch, mainly by selling Jack's writings both in print worldwide and through film contracts. She travelled frequently to Europe until 1939, the beginning or World War II, to work with agents, publishers and translators, as well as to give talks in public and on radio. As a result,she became a well known personality in her own right.

Charmian never remarried although she had a few relationships with men. Despite a serious horseback accident in 1935, she rode well into her seventies. She supported prison reform and animal welfare activities. By 1940 she was suffering minor strokes and eventually died in January 1955 at 84 years of age. Her ashes were placed alongside Jack's as she had requested. A local newspaper described her best: "Her engaging smile, her splendid intellect, the eternal life she gave to Jack London".

Mercedes López-Tomlinson
Director
Trotamundas Press

" A sense of marvel drifts to me—
Of morning on a purple sea,
And fragrant islands far away."

—GEORGE STERLING.

FOREWORD

' JACK LONDON and Hawaii ! '' From the years of his youth the two names have been entwined in the minds of those who knew him best—since that day when, bound for the Japan sealing grounds and Behring Sea on the *Sophie Suther-land* (the schooner " Ghost " of *The Sea Wolf*), he first glimpsed to northward the smoke and fire of Kilauea. Through successive visits, including eighteen months spent in the islands during the last two years of his life, through early misunderstanding and final loving comprehension of him, Jack London and Hawaii have drawn together, with increasing devotion in his heart for " Aloha-Land "—" Love-Land," in his fashion of speech—until at the end he could answer to the long-desired appellation, kamaaina, one-who-belongs, and more.

" They don't know what they've got ! " he said of the American public, when, a decade ago, headed for the South Seas in his own small-boat voyage around the world, he sailed far out of his course that Hawaii might be the first port of call, and threw himself into learning the mani-

9

fold beauty and wonder of this territory of Uncle
Sam. And "They don't know what they've
got," he repeated to each new unscrolling of
its wonder and beauty during five months of
enjoyment and study of land and people. Again
in Hawaii after the breaking out of the Great
War, he amended: " Because they have no
other place to go, they are just beginning to
realize what they've got."

And really, the knowledge of the citizen of the
States is woefully scant concerning this possession but a few days distant by steamer, and
woefully he distorts its very name in conversation and song into something like Haw-way'-ah.
To the adept in the lovely language there are
fine nuances in the vowelly word ; but simple
Hah-wy'-ee serves well.

What does the average middle-aged American
know of the amazing history of this amazing
" native " people now voting as American
citizens ? The name Hawaii calls to memory
vague dots on a soiled map of the Pacific Ocean,
bearing a vaguely gastronomic caption that in
no wise reminds him of the Earl of Sandwich,
Lord of the British Admiralty, and patron of
the intrepid discoverer, Captain Cook, whose
valiant bones even now rest on the Kona
Coast. Savage, remote, alluring, adventurous,
are the impressions ; but few have grasped the
fact that that pure Polynesian, Kamehameha
the Great, deserved to rank as one of the most
remarkable figures in history for his revolutionary

genius, unaided by outland ideas, and who, dying in 1819, little more than a year before the first missionaries sailed from Boston, had fought his way to the consolidation under one Government of the group of eight islands, ended feudal monarchy, abolished idolatry, and all unknowing made the land ripe for Christian civilization.

Of those whom I have questioned, only one ever heard that, before this generation, indeed previous to the discovery of gold in California and the starting of our forebears over the plains by ox-team or across the Isthmus of Panama, early settlers in California were sending their children to be educated in the excellent missionary schools of these isles of inconsequential name, and importing their wheat from the same " savage " port.

In this journal covering a few months spent ten years ago in Hawaii, concluding with a résumé of experiences there in 1915-1916, I have tried to limn a picture of the charm of the Hawaiian islander as he was, and is becoming, with the enchantment of his lofty isles, and their abundant hospitality.

During the original writing many elisions were advised by Jack London, as being too personal of himself for me, being me, to publish. However, in the circumstances of his untimely passing, and in view of a desire made evident to me in countless letters as well as in the press, for biographical work, I have been led to reinstate and elaborate much of the mass of data. Even in face of his objections at the time, I had stoutly disagreed, maintaining that the lovers of his soul and his work would value revelation of his personality and manner of living life.

And so, missing incalculably the grace of his final censorship, I am chancing the test. If the personal pronoun I too lavishly peppers the story, take the rôle of "the gentle reader" toward me, I pray, and consider the inevitable handicap of one who writes intimately of a dear and gracious subject.

CHARMIAN KITTREDGE LONDON.

GLEN ELLEN, CALIFORNIA,
IN THE VALLEY OF THE MOON,
September 1, 1917.

JACK LONDON AND HAWAII

PEARL HARBOUR, OAHU,
TERRITORY OF HAWAII,
Tuesday, May 21, 1907.

COME tread with me a little space of Paradise. Many pleasant acres have I trod hitherto, but never an acre like this. It is so beautiful. And restful. And green. Green upon green. With blue-depthed shadows imposed from green depthed foliage of great trees upon thick deep lawn that cushions underfoot. Bare foot. For one somehow dissociates the idea of footwear with an acre of Elysium. It is one of the paradisal blessings of this new Sweet Home of ours that we may blissfully pace it unshod, and for the most part unobserved.

The street is a mere white, meandering, coral-powdered byway ; nothing less inquisitive than the birds abides in the adjoining garden, where a rustic dwelling shows but vaguely amidst a riot of foliage ; and on our southern boundary is a tropic tangle of uninhabited wildwood, fronting upon a native fish-pond—an elongated bit of bay enclosed by a low wall of masonry of such antiquity that no tradition of Hawaii can place its origin.

Bayward the outlook is a rosy coral-reef, swept by the tepid pea-green tides ; and to its outer rim extends a slender wooden jetty, at the end of which our ship's-boat can lie even, at low tide.

An eighth of a mile beyond in the rippling chryso-prase flood of Pearl Harbour, " Dream Harbour " Jack loves to call it, swings our Boat of Dreams —our little *Snark*, anchored in the first port of call on her mission of pure golden adventure—a gallant foolishness, perhaps, but if we be fools, let us be gallant ones. Whenever my happy eyes come to rest on her shining shape, I feel them growing big with visions of the coming years on her deck ; and then, remembering vivid incidents of the voyage, I drift back to the lovely earth with a filling sense of several laps of adventure already run. Not the least of these is mere living in a green shady nook of Paradise where one's eyes must quest twice in the green gloom among enormous trees to discover near the water-side the habitation—a very small, very rustic, very simple brown bungalow of three rooms—only one, our big breezy bedroom, quite deserving of the name of room. The others are, one, a long and narrow seaward strip like an enclosed veranda ; the other, a cosy cubby of a kitchen. A tin pantry, an ample bathroom, and windows, windows everywhere, make per-fect the indoor aspect of this Arcadian acre.

Already, in swimming suits, we have ventured the reef at high tide, with unbounded delight in the sunwashed liquid silk. Our goal for to-morrow is the yacht, informed as we are that there is little danger of man-eating sharks in this sheltered harbour.

Beyond the *Snark*, across this arm of the sea, over low green volcanic hills lying south-east between Pearl Lochs and Honolulu, one is just able to glimpse the rosy bulk of Diamond Head, dreaming in the fervent sunlight. To the north, over vast rice-fields, and upland plantations, shrug the rugged, riven Kolau Loa Mountains, their heads lost in heavy cloud-masses that seem everlastingly to roll and shift above these tropic ranges.

Pearl Harbour embraces some twelve square miles, divided naturally into three lochs, or arms of the sea, by two peninsulas, on the eastern of which lies the village dignified by the suggestive name of Pearl City. Trust me for having already possessed myself of the knowledge that the locality has been these many years filched of its jewels.

On the south-eastern extremity of our particular " neck of the woods " stray a few suburban homes of the Honolulans, of which ours is one. Tochigi, Nipponese and poet-browed cabin-boy of the *Snark*, will live ashore with us and resume his erstwhile household service, while the rest of the yacht's complement—Roscoe, sailing-master, Bert, engineer of our ruined machinery, and Martin, cook because there was no other berth vacant—will retain their accommodations aboard. In these protected waters the boat lies at least as steady as a house on wheels, as she swings to ebb and flow.

Strangely content are we in the unwonted tranquillity of motion and sound, lacking wish to venture afield, even to Honolulu a scant twelve miles distant by the railroad. Enough just to rest and rest, and gaze around upon the beautiful, long-desired world of island. Scarcely can we glance athwart the apple-green water but there curves a span of rainbow between our eyes and the far hills, and like as not a double-span, with promise of a triple-bow; while frequent warm showers delicately veil the land's vivid emerald with all-melting tints of opal.

Very florid, all this, you will smile—a bit overdone, perhaps? Gird at my word-storms if you will. Then consider, and take ship for this "fleet of islands" in the western ocean. It isn't real; it can't be—too sweet it is, day and night, the round twenty-four hours. Here but the one night and day, already we grope for new forms of expression, as will you an you follow the sinking sun.

The heat is not oppressive, even though the season is close to summer. But one must realize that Hawaii is only sub-tropical. To be precise, the group of eight inhabited islands occupies a central position in the North Pacific, and lies just within the northern tropic. For the benefit of any sailor who may run and read, Jack says I might as well be still more explicit, and record that the *Snark*, anchored about 2000

sea miles south-west of her native shore, lies
between 18° 54' and 22° 15' north latitude, and
between 154° 50' and 160° 30' of longitude west
of Greenwich. Figures never did stick with
me—there seems to be a positive lack in my brain,
that is the despair of my thoroughly mathe-
matical and practical commander, who can
reduce anything in the world to his eternal
" arithmetic." (*Almost* anything, I hear him
disavow, for none so humble as he to offer that
there are holy things of the human heart and
mind far from amenable to rule of thumb.)
What does penetrate my senses in this particular
case is the immutable truth that this ocean
paradise is blessed with a lower temperature
than any other country in the same latitude.
The reasons are simple enough—the prevailing
" orderly trades " that blow over a large extent
of the ocean, and the ocean itself that is cooled
by the return current from the region of Bering
Straits. Pleasantly warm though we found the
waters of Pearl Harbour this bright morning,
yet are they less warm by ten degrees than the
waters of other regions in similar latitudes.

And now, to go back a little and recount how we
came to rest in this fair haven—Fair Haven, in
passing, was the name bestowed upon Honolulu
Harbour by one of her discoverers, Captain
Brown, when, in 1794, in his schooner *Jackal*, in
company with Captain Gordon in the sloop
Prince Lee Boo, he entered the bay, and mixed
in local affairs by selling arms and ammunition

to King Kalanikupule of Oahu, then resisting
an invasion from the sovereign of the island of
Maui, Kaeo. Right near us here, at Kalauao
on the way to Honolulu, a red battle was waged,
in which Kalanikupule, assisted by Captain
Brown and his men, overcame the powerful
enemy.

Poor Captain Brown was born unlucky, it would
seem. Firing a salute the next day from the
Jackal, in honour of the victory, a wad from
his guns went wild and killed Captain Ken-
drick, who was quietly dining aboard his own
vessel, the *Lady Washington*. The blameless
skipper's funeral, being of a different sort from
the native ceremony, was believed by the Hawaiians to constitute an act of sorcery to induce
the death of Captain Brown. Kalanikupule paid
the latter 400 hogs for his valorous part in the
struggle with the vanquished Kaeo, and Brown,
after the sailing of the *Lady Washington* for
China, put his men to salting down the valuable
pork at Kaihikapu, an ancient salt pond between
Pearl Harbour and Honolulu.

One day while the *Jackal's* mate, Mr. Lamport,
and the sailors were gathering salt, Kamohomoho,
uncle of Oahu's king, boarded the *Prince Lee
Boo* and the *Jackal*, and more than made good
the " act of sorcery " by dispatching poor
Brown as well as Gordon, imprisoning those of
the crews not employed ashore. Lamport and
his men were captured, but their lives spared.
The gratitude of the royal family for favours

rendered had been out-balanced by ambition for a modern navy with which to attack Kamehameha the Great on the " Big Island," Hawaii. On the voyage, however, the white seamen regained possession of the vessels, sent the natives ashore in their own canoes which were being towed, and lost no time following the *Lady Washington* to the Orient.

But I become lost in the fascinating history of the men who blazed our trail to these romantic isles, and forget that this is a chronicle of a more modern adventure.

On the mainland, before sailing out through the Golden Gate, we made the fortunate acquaintance of one, Mr. Thomas W. Hobron, artist, merchant, good fellow, and citizen of Honolulu, who spoke in this wise : " I wonder if you two would care to put up in my little shack on the peninsula ? It isn't much to look at, and there's only room enough for the two of you ; but it's brimful of Aloha, if you care to use it."

So here are we, blessing good Tom Hobron, as we shall bless him all our years, for the gift of so idyllic a resting-spot after the tumult of our first traverse on the bit of boat yonder.

And yet, casting back over those twenty-six days of ceaseless tossing, we are aware only of pleasure in the memory of every least happening, disagreeable and agreeable alike. In fact the last week aboard was so cosy and homelike that more than often we caught ourselves regretting the imminent termination of the cruise. Even

at this moment of writing, despite blissful surroundings, did I not know that the *Snark's* dear
adventures were but just begun, I should be robbed
indeed, so in love am I with sea and *Snark* :—

For the wind and waterways have stamped me with their
    seal.

We picked up a good slant of wind to make
Honolulu yesterday morning—an immeasurable
relief after the wearisome calm of the night
before, during which we had taken our turns
at the idle wheel and scanned the contrary
compass with all emotions, of anxiety, while
the helpless yacht swung on every arc of the circle, with no slightest fan of air to fill the limp sails
that flapped heavily in the glassy off-shore
heave. Never shall I forget my own tense
double-watch of four hours, straining eye and ear
toward the all-too-nigh coral reefs off Koho Head,
with Mokopuu Point light blinking to the north-
east. But when a dart of sun through a deck-
light woke me from brief sleep, we were spank-
ing along smartly in a cobalt sea threshed white
on every rushing wave, with the green and gold
island of Oahu shifting its scenery like a sliding
screen as we swept past lovely rose-tawny
Diamond Head and palm-dotted Waikiki toward Honolulu Harbour. After an oddly fish-
less voyage of four weeks, we were joyously
excited over a school of big porpoises, " puffing-
pigs," intent as any flock of barnyard fowl to
cross our fleeing forefoot. Undignified haste was

their only resemblance to domestic poultry, for in general movement they were more like sportive colts hurdling in pasture with snort and puff —sleek sides glistening blue-black in the brilliant sunlight.

To our land-eager eyes the beautiful old city was the surpassing picture of her pictures as, still outside, we came abreast of her wharves—the water-front with ships and steamers moored beside the long sheds ; and, behind, the Pompeian-red Punch Bowl, so often described by early voyagers ; the suburban heights of Tantalus ; the purple-deep rifts of valleys and gorges ; and the green-and-violet needled peaks upthrusting through dense dark cloud wrack.

Barely had we finished Martin's eggless breakfast when a Government launch frothed alongside, and the engineer's cheery " Want a line, Jack—eh ? " sounded classic assurance of Hawaii's far-famed grace of hospitality. Since despite my sanguine temperament, I had been conscious of a premonition that something unfortunate would happen upon our arrival, probably due to the impression left by the hasty ship-chandler of San Francisco who unjustly libelled the *Snark* in Oakland and delayed our sailing. So this easy and gracious " Want a line, Jack ? " was music to my ears. You see, Jack London is not infrequently arrested, or nearly arrested, for one reason or another, whenever he sets his merry foot upon foreign soil (I have disquieting memories of Cuba, Japan, and Korea) ; and Hawaii *seems* like foreign soil, albeit annexed by the Stars and Stripes.

The morning paper, the *Pacific Commercial Advertiser*, preceded Immigration Inspector Brown and Customs Inspector Farmer over the rail, and they laughingly pointed to a conspicuously leaded item that the *Snark* was supposed to be lost with all on board—bright tidings already cabled to California and read by our horrified families and friends ! We cannot help wishing we were early enough here to be handed the very first English newspaper published at Honolulu, in 1836—the *Sandwich Islands Gazette*. And two years before that the Hawaiian sheets, *Kumu Hawaii* and *Lama Hawaii*, were the first newspapers issued in the Pacific Ocean.

Speed is not the object of our junketing in the Seven Seas ; but if we of the *Snark* had known any hurt vanity about the length of our passage, it would have been amply offset by the report the Inspectors made of the big bark *Edward May* arriving six days before, which beat our tardy record but two days, after an equally uneventful voyage.

Meanwhile the pilot had come aboard, a line was passed for'ard to the launch, and we now ripped and zipped over a billowy swell to meet the Port Physician, Dr. Sinclair, whose white launch could be seen putting out from a wharf. That dignitary, once on deck, scanned our clean Bill of Health, asked a few routine questions—one of which was whether we carried any rats or snakes ;

and all three officials pronounced us free to enter the Port of Honolulu. Whereupon Jack stated that we were bound for Pearl Lochs, expecting there to find Mr. Tom Hobron, and was in return informed by the pilot that Mr. Hobron had been called to San Francisco for an indefinite period, but that he knew the cottage was at our disposal in accordance with the understanding. Furthermore, we were smilingly told that the wharves of Honolulu were lined with her citizens, waiting to garland us in welcome; but too strong behind our eyes was the fancied picture of the promised retreat by the still waters of Pearl Lochs, so we thanked our kind visitors, secured a launch, and towed resolutely past the hospitable city.

" It does seem a darned shame," Jack mused regretfully. " But what can we do with all our plans made for Pearl Harbour ? And anyway," he added, " I don't want the general public to see boat of mine sail in, looking as if she'd been half-built and then half-wrecked, the way this one does . . . I've got *some* pride."

Then all attention was claimed by the beauty of our westward way to the harbour entrance, as we closely skirted a broad shoreward reef where greenest breakers combed and burst into fountains of tourmaline and turquoise, shot through with javelins of sun-gold, and the air was filled with rainbow mist. Our boat slipped along in a world compounded of the very ravishment of melting colours—land and sea, it was

all of a piece ; while off to the south-eastern horizon ocean and sky merged in palest silvery
azure, softly gloomed by shadowy shapes of other
Promised Islands.

Turning almost due north into the narrow reef-
entrance to the Lochs, we could easily have sailed
unassisted, even with the light breeze then re-
maining, so well marked is the channel which has
been dredged, full thirty feet deep, to admit passage of the largest vessels into this land-locked
harbour, invaluable acquisition to the American
Government.   Its low green banks show both
lava and coral formation, and vast cane plantations and gently terraced rice-fields slope their
green leagues back to the foothills of the Waianae
Mountains.   Scattered over the rice-areas are
picturesquely tattered Mongolians, who utter
long resonant calls to frighten the marauding
rice-birds, which, floating up in black, disturbed
clouds, are brought down with shotguns.

We two, with oneness in love of our watery
roaming, were happy and vociferous as a pair
of children, entering this our first port.   Had
we given it a thought, we could have wished for
a less civilized landfall, with conscious missing
of a native face or two.   But I am sure this never
entered our blissful heads—not mine, at any
rate ; and my memory of Jack's alert and beaming face precludes doubt of his contentment with
things as they were.

Presently, as we wound along between the western peninsula and a little green islet, he called

attention to the snowy bore of a tiny craft racing towards us from ahead. In short order a
smart white launch was rounding up with dash
and style befitting the commodore of the famed
Hawaiian Yacht Club, Mr. Clarence Macfarlane,
who, with Mr. Albert Waterhouse, a neighbour
of this little eastern peninsula of ours, had
learned by telephone from Honolulu of our arrival,
and hurried out to make us welcome. Both of
these " dandy fellows," as Jack promptly rated
them, sent a warm glow through us by the un-
assuming goodwill of their greeting eyes and
hearty hand-grasp, while the first words on their
lips was the beautiful Hawaiian " *Aloha !* "
(ah-lo-hah) that is epitome of all goodwill and
unquestioning friendship. No noise nor flurry
was theirs, as they set foot for the first time
on the deck of the much-bruited *Snark*; only
the kindest, quietest, make-yourself-at-home
manner, as if we had all been acquainted for
years, or else that it was the most usual thing
in the world to receive a wild man and woman
who had essayed to circumnavigate the globe in
an absurd small shallop of outlandish rig. But
those keen sailor eyes, all the while we were being made welcome to Hawaii, missed jot nor tittle
of the vessel's lines and visible equipment, for
to the mind of the world at large this boat of
ours, " the strongest of her size ever built," to
quote her owner, with convenient English Dogger
Bank sail-plan, is a somewhat questionable experiment. I caught Albert Waterhouse's rov-

ing eye on its return from examining the stepping
of the stout mizzenmast, which stepping constitutes the main difference between our imported
ketch-rig and the more familiar yawl; and
the comprehending laugh in my own eyes called
out a roguish half-embarrassed twinkle in his.
But " Zing ! she's some boat ! " he appreciated,
as he took in the sturdy sticks and teak deck-
fittings, and the general compactness of our forty-
five by fifteen foot ocean home.

And then he told how he had been commissioned
by Tom Hobron to turn over the bungalow and
do what he could to make us at home. His
first neighbourly service was to see the *Snark*
properly anchored off the Hobron jetty, the while
I strained my eyes across the eighth-mile of grey-
green water to glimpse the " not-much-to-look-
at ' shack ' " amongst the plumy depths of
foliage.

Leaving the crew aboard to make everything
snug, Jack and I were carried by launch farther
up the Loch to a long wooden foot pier that
leads over the shallow shore-reef to a spacious
suburban place where live Albert Waterhouse
and his little family.

And here occurred a teapotful of mischance.
Let none question that negotiating several hundred
feet of narrow, stationary, unrailed bridge above
shifting water, by legs that for over three weeks
have known only a pitching surface of forty-five
by fifteen, is little short of tragedy for one who
would make seeming entry into a hospitable

strange land. I know how Jack looked; I can only tell how I felt. And he was distinctly unkind. He made no secret of his amusement at my astonishing gyrations, although to my jaundiced eye his own progress was equally open to criticism.

It still puzzles, how I ever traversed the distance without a ducking. Repeatedly I had to apologize to Mr. Waterhouse or Commodore Macfarlane for the frantic dabs made at them to prevent myself from going headlong into the water. It was outrageous, the way that interminable board-walk would rise straight up until I felt obliged to lean acutely forward to the ascent, in terror of bumping a sunburnt nose—only to find that it had abruptly slanted downward, whereupon I must angle as giddily backward to preserve a becoming balance. From the rear, Jack, in difficulties of his own, tittered something about his wife's " sad walk," and I remember retorting with asperity that it was a pity he had never noticed it before. Then we all fell to laughing and, very much better acquainted for the fun, somehow gained the coral-gravelled path-way that led into a garden of green lawns, hedged by scarlet-blooming shrubbery, and shaded by great gnarled trees that would have delighted Doré's tortured imagination.

In respose to her husband's shout of " Here they are, Gretchen ! I've got 'm ! Zing ! " Mrs. Waterhouse, a cool and unruffled vision of woman, moved toward us on bare sandalled

feet across the broad shaded veranda of the
big cool house, a stately figure in long unbroken lines of sheer muslin and lace.

" You poor child," ,was her greeting to me,
with arm-around hovering me into a white bathroom all sweet-scented and piled with fluffy
towels. " You must be nearly tired to death,
I can just imagine how I'd feel after such a trip !
Just come right in here and rest your bones
in a good hot bath before lunch."

Rightly she guessed our tired bones ; and
rightly she prescribed the beneficence of steaming water. But the ache was from the violent
stresses in accommodating our precious skeletons
to a stable environment, rather than from any
hardships of sea-buffeting. Fifteen minutes' relaxation in that shining tub made me all new ;
and, once more in my blue silk bloomer-suit, I
joined the happy captain of my boat and heart.
Likewise bathed and refreshed (his wet hair
wickedly though futilely brushed to snub the
curling ends), sprawled in cool white ducks
upon a broad flat couch spread deep with fine-
woven native mats, he was immersed in a magazine of later date than our sailing from California. No one was about for the moment, and we
lay and looked around with wordless content in
this, our first household of Hawaii. Everything
was restfully shaded, yet nothing dark, what of
the light polished floors, light walls, and handsome rattan furniture. Roomy window-seats,
banked with cushions, lovely pictures, and a

" baby-grand " piano, furnished an air of city elegance to the equally refined summer rusticity. I did not even want to touch the alluring piano ; to lie deep in that reclining chair of cool rattan and to know that it was there, golden-complete within its glossy casing, was all-satisfying.

Jack, watching under his long lashes, smiled indulgently.

" Funny way to make a living, Mate-Woman ! " Often he thinks aloud about his selection of a means of livelihood, and ever grows more convinced that he chose the best of all ways for him—and me. " I carry my office in my head, and see the world while I earn the money to see it with." And verily have my lines fallen in pleasant places, the garner from a congenial artistry making accessible those pleasant places.

And here entered Gretchen Waterhouse, with her lovely babe in her arms, breathing beauty and comfort and cleanliness—such a sumptuous Germanic Madonna, with heavy hair parted smoothly over placid deep-blue eyes and wide low brow, and piled high in a smooth tower. She was followed by that mischievous-eyed husband of hers, who announced luncheon with a jolly : " Come on, you famished seafarers, and see what there is to eat ! " But first we must be crowned, I with a wreath of small pink roses, dainty as a string of coral, while around Jack's neck was laid a wide circlet of limp green vine, glossy and fragrant. Commodore Macfarlane was also decorated in the same charming way that the white dwellers of the Islands have adopted from the sweet native custom.

The meal was furnished forth on a side veranda, or *lanai* (lahn-I) as they say here, screened with flowering vines, and our host and hostess were on tiptoe to see whether or not we would be " good sports " in trying the native dishes which form part of their daily menu. As Jack said afterward, they " let us down easy," because, instead of experimenting on our *malihini* (new-comer) palates with straight *poi*, Albert Water-house diluted some of the smooth pinkish-grey paste with cold water and milk, and added a pinch of salt. Served in a long thin glass, he called this a poi cocktail. I scarcely see how any one could dislike it. The plain thick poi, unseasoned, would be debatable to those unfor-tunates who dread sampling anything " odd " ; but we took to it instanter. It must have ex-cellent food value, being as it is the staple of all Pacific native peoples who are lucky enough to have right conditions for its raising. They showed us how to combine the plain poi with accessories—a spoonful of the cool grey mush with a bite of meat or salt dried fish. Eaten by itself, poi is somewhat flat in taste, like slightly fermented starch. I do not know whether they were joking, but our friends told us that it is used successfully for wall-paper paste ! In these days poi is manufactured by machinery in nice sanitary factories. Originally it was made by first roasting the tuber of the taro plant, wrapped in leaves, among hot stones in the ground, then pounding the malleable mass with stone poi-pounders and manipulating it with the hands. It would be noteworthy if foot-work had not also been utilized, as by the Italians in macaroni-making.

Also we were regaled with the tuber itself, fresh boiled, a very good vegetable, prepared like a potato, with butter, salt, and pepper. It would be hard to give an idea of the flavour, and so many writers have failed to describe foreign tastes that as yet I am not going to try, save to state that I feel sure taro would prove a satisfactory substitute for both bread and potatoes, if one were deprived of the old stand-bys.

Following the leisurely luncheon, Jack was interviewed by several perspiring newspaper men who had taken the first train to Pearl City after the elusive *Snark* had passed out of sight ; and in the mid-afternoon Mr. Waterhouse accompanied us to our new dwelling, distant about ten minutes' walk. We met the entire crew bound for the village to see what they could see. Even the gentle Tochigi was bitten by the popular sight-seeing bug. And Tochigi, alas, failed to return until evening, so that I was obliged to do the unpacking. For Jack had developed a vicious headache, and I hastened to reduce all confusion and establish a serene home atmosphere ; but I must confess that the really happy task was an uphill one, when it wasn't downhill, due to the sad walk that led me devious ways and many extra steps, with frequent halts to orient a revolving brain.

By seven, with still no Tochigi, and not a scrap to eat, came a tap on the door. As if in answer to a wish, there stood a smiling woman bearing a tray of enormous tomatoes and cucumbers, a neatly napkined loaf of freshly baked bread, and a generous pat of home-made butter. She is our nearest neighbour, Miss Frances Johnson, with whom, upon a suggestion from Mrs. Waterhouse, we have this day made arrangements to board.

No sooner had she gone than a cousin of Mr. Waterhouse brought an offering of *papaias* (pah-py'-ahs)—wonderful green-and-yellow melon things that grow on trees—and asked what further he could do for us. The combination of old-world and new-world neighbourliness was quite overwhelming, and I was more than grateful, for by now poor Jack had taken to the big white bed, although he weakly admitted that he might eat a tomato if urged.

Alas, for wifely solicitude. Old Ocean played a wicked trick. As I was nearing the pallid sufferer's bedside with a plateful of big red slices, which I had dressed with lemon and oil as he likes them, something distracted my attention, and I made to set the dish on a table. The house lurched and the floor gave a sickening jerk, and I actually missed the table. Of course the salad splashed on the floor, in a havoc of shattered porcelain. I do not know exactly what this particular confession is " good " for, but I might as well confess wholly while I am about it. A second salad was made, and—it went the way of the first. My sea-legs refused to stiffen into land-legs in one day, and little help they received from my eyes accustomed to shifting surroundings. Besides, I was dead tired. When the second plate broke on the floor, the giggle that smothered Jack's " Poor little kid ! " robbed me of pity for the painful shaking the giggle caused him.

Now that I am into the subject of Jack's illness, this day of his first landfall, with his permission I am going to divulge the cause. In fact, he mentioned it himself to one of the harbour officials this morning. And anyway, he is the frankest human being concerning his frailties that ever I knew. The majority of civilized humanity, being trained from without and within to repress their faults or peccadilloes, fail to comprehend this ingenuously open attitude. He is so candid that they think, without thinking, that he must be concealing something. Pardon the double paradox, but it seems to express what I am after. For example : if, in an autobiographical sketch or article, he mentions having been arrested, whether as boy-tramp or as war-correspondent, his charitable compeers of the press proceed to brand him as indisputably a jail-bird and criminal " who should be behind

B

the bars " ; or, if he tells the thrilling tale of how, as a mere youth in the Klondyke, he shot the notoriously difficult White Horse Rapids with a glass of whisky in him, up goes a hue and cry about the pity of Jack London being a hopeless drunkard ! Please believe, I am not exaggerating.

But to the case in point. Jack was thirtyone last January, and had smoked cigarettes ever since he was somewhere around fourteen. And when I say smoked, I mean smoked. He smoked all his waking hours—in the daytime, at work or at play, at night when reading and studying, stocking his remarkable brain with knowledge of every kind. His mind is like a library of infinite shelves, where he is endlessly cataloguing contributions from every source. Once, only, had I ever broached the subject of smoking—two years ago, shortly before we were wedded. From the conversation we held, swinging in a hammock under the laurels at Wake Robin Lodge, I seemed to gather that his smoking habit was a rather negligible detail in comparison with the thousand and one larger issues that occupied his mind. How shall I say ?—that this habit, a mere habit, which takes none of his conscious attention in its pursuance, should not be too seriously considered by him or others. This roughly is the most I could conclude at the time, as to his outlook upon smoking in so far as concerned himself ; and, having firmly philosophized these many years that my " not impossible he " should never be nagged, I had permitted myself no further reference to the ubiquitous cigarette. However, I did notice, during our months in the country, that occasionally he would restrict himself to only just several a day, say on our long horseback jaunts through Northern California ; and, once, with a certain rare little half-bashful smile that sits quaintly beneath the calm sweet of his grey eyes, he said : " I'm really trying to cut down a little, you see."

That was all ; and never a word to me passed his lips until we cleared the Golden Gate that he intended to forego his nerve-soothing custom on the passage to Hawaii. Naturally I was delighted at the well-executed surprise ; but I hid my misgivings as to the contentment of his nervous system under the unescapable shock of cutting off so abruptly the narcotic of seventeen years. Keenly as he felt the need at times, nevertheless it never once made him visibly irritable. Once or twice, he told me a couple of weeks out, he suffered from an illusion that there were cigarettes aboard if only he could find them, and that the rest of us were concealing them from him. His continual joy in the voyage went far to offset the deprivation, and after a little he ceased to miss his " Imperiales." But when the Customs officer yesterday boarded the *Snark*, my young skipper immediately asked for a cigarette, with an " I'm going to see how it tastes." It did not taste " just right " and he tried another—and several. In short, as the day wore, poor Jack found himself suffering with as absurd intensity as any surreptitious small limb of Satan during his first smoke. He was just merely " laid out " to quote his own words ; and be it accredited to my good page that I did not giggle at his plight as he did when his second salad lapsed redly upon the floor.

At length he fell sound asleep under the well-tucked cloud of find bobinet that graces all Hawaiian beds (the mosquito seems to be the serpent of this Eden), and I breathed a sigh of relief, having this long time learned that sleep is the only medicine for any brand of a J. L. head-ache. Also, I was desperately weary, I might say land-sick, and more than ready to turn in upon my chosen canopied cot in a breezy corner of the big room.

My troubles had only begun.

When the crew passed through on their return to the yacht, I softly called Martin to look at the kitchen-sink faucet, which was not working properly. As soon as he turned on the water, up wriggled a truly appalling centipede all of five inches in length. The leathery toughness of the monstrous insect, which was as thick as my finger, made the slaying of it an eminently lively and disgusting tussle. Martin finally vanquished the leggy foe, but we kept a wary eye for its possible mate. Fate left it to me, alone in the bathroom—for I would not disturb Jack's healing slumbers—to deal with the mate. After scissoring off its ugly fanged head, I fled to bed, fer-

vently trusting to dream of things with wings—
birds, butterflies, angels. No remembered assur-
ances of the very mild venomousness of this
transplanted little dragon can ever lessen its
hideous offensiveness. In my mind there is filed
away a word of protest for its every leg, of which,
despite its name, I counted but seventy-four.
The people here pay little attention to this insect's
bite.

In the morning I told Tochigi to remove the
mutilated remains. Oh, of course, they must be
displayed to an admiring audience of husband
before cremation; I had no call to forego the
praise of his " Plucky kid ! " For even more
fussy is he than I, about crawly things, and he
could see, by involuntary reminiscent tremors,
that my overworn nerves had been somewhat
shaken by the encounter. Not having laughed
at me, we could laugh in company later in the
morning, when, hair-brush in hand, he went
right into the air, with a " Great Scot ! " before
an ill-looking hairy grey spider, some four or five
inches across, that dropped from the ceiling and
clattered upon the bureau-top. Was it Mark
Twain who was disturbed at his writing by one
of these, and put the cuspidor upon it, claiming
that a grey fringe of legs showed all around the
vessel ? Somewhere I had read that these
spiders are descendants of the tarantula ; but
they have descended a long way, for the tarantulas
that taught caution to my Southern California
childhood were meaty monsters compared with

these paper-and-fuzz household gods of Hawaii, which harm nothing more serious than mosquitoes and other dispensable insects.

Jack had slept off the headache, and was able to enjoy his first luncheon at Miss Johnson's. (Tochigi is to cook our light breakfast at home). Miss Johnson and her sisters, Miss Ellen and Mrs. Fyfe, served a most appetizing table for us sea-worn pilgrims—a capital steak, done rare to a nicety, accompanied by taro which had been boiled and then sliced and fried slightly in fresh butter; big cool platefuls of raw tomatoes and cucumbers in oil and lemon; poi, with dried salt *aku* (ah-koo), bonita, papaias, avocados, the almost prohibitively expensive alligator-pears that we know in California, where they are sent by steamer and in shipping deteriorate; and bananas so luscious that we declared we had never before' tasted bananas. These and sweet seedling oranges, as well as papaias, thrive in the fragrant garden of roses and hibiscus and palms, seen through the venetian blinds from where we sat at table, eating hothouse viands in the hot-house air.

We came away congratulating ourselves and each other upon such a feasting place within two minutes' walk of our own little red gate; and the trio of ladies granted indulgence to drop over in any garmenture that pleases our mood, and also offered the piano for my use at any hour. Although even on this warm leeward side of Oahu the temperature is said to range only from 60° to 85°, with a mean of 74°, the humid quality of the atmosphere makes one much more content in loose lines of apparel. Yesterday it was ducks and bloomers for Jack and me. This morning it was ducks and a summer lawn. But this afternoon, in the dreamy green privacy of our lovely acre, it is kimono and kimono, thank you, with not much else to mention. And I am already planning certain flowing gowns of muslin and lace, on the pattern of Gretchen Waterhouse's home attire, which flouncy robe is called a *holoku*. It is a worthy development from the first clothing introduced by the missionaries, the simplest known design—like that cut by our childhood scissors for paper dolls, and called *muumuu* (moo-oo-moo-oo smoothly) by the Hawaiians. In time this evolved into the full Mother Hubbard atrocity; but in this year of grace (thank the stars for that grace!) it is a sumptuous, swinging, trailing model of its own, just escaping the curse of the Mother Hubbard and somehow eluding the significance of wrapper. Not all women would look as well in the holoku as does Mrs. Albert, who is straight and tall and walks as if with pride in her fine height and proportion, as large women should walk. I believe a great measure of the holoku's good looks depends upon its being carried well. The muumuu, in its pristine simplicity, is still used by native women for an undergarment, and, in all colours of calico, for swimming, although I have yet to learn how it could permit any freedom of movement in the water.

"It hasn't taken you long to size up the styles in Hawaii," Jack smiled to me just now, after I had read him the above. But he added, appreciatively: "I hope you will get some of those loose white things. I like them."

Paucity of coast mail would indicate that relatives and friends have been chary of wasting energy on letters that might never be received by such reckless rovers. O ye of scant faith in the *Snark's* oaken ribs and her owner's canny judgment! Not so with me, who am most concerned, after him, in the safety of the venture. Laying aside personal bias, there is not another man in the round world with whom I should care to risk my precious neck in a deep-sea vessel of the *Snark's* measurements, because of Jack's lifelong experience in *small*-boat sailing, a branch of sailor-knowledge that stands by itself. Many's the gold-braided, grand old captain of great liners, who knows little or nothing of the handling of small sailing craft. Many's the deep-water seaman on big ships who is equally ignorant of the ways of small boats. But the sailor man who knows both kinds, pronounces: "Give me the small boat, every time, for safety at sea! She stays on top! And she rides one wave at a time!"

In addition to first-hand education in sailboats on San Francisco Bay, which unreliable sheet of water he knows from end to end, and seven months at sea in the *Sophie Sutherland*, Jack is possessed of swift right judgment in emergency. For many years I have yachted on the water-ways of California, so little known except to river dwellers and fishermen, and several times with Jack at the helm of his old sloop *Spray*, and never have I seen his equal for correlation of mind and body. All this for the doubting ones who curtail their unenthusiastic epistles to us of the *Snark*.

The mail was brought by a tiny " jerk water " bobtail dummy and coach run by one, Tony, from Pearl City, a mile away, to a station near the end of the peninsula. Tony is a handsome little swarthy fellow, regarded by me with much interest, as my first Hawaiian on his native heath. Certain misgivings at sight of him rendered my surprise less to learn that he is full-blooded Portuguese. Alack, my first Hawaiian is a Portuguese—and of course Jack is hilarious.

One other caller crossed the springy turf of our garden—Bert's uncle, Mr. Rowell of Honolulu, who, having been told we were looking for saddle animals, came to suggest that we bring up our saddles the first of next week, and ride two of his horses back to the peninsula, where we are welcome to them as long as we please. Truly, the face of Hawaii hospitality is fair to see. What a place to live, with the gift of a roof from the rain, tree-tops from the noon-day sun, a peaceful space in which to work, strange pleasant foods irreproachably set forth, a warm vast bowl of jade for our swimming, and fleet steeds for less than the asking ! As this latest gift-bringer departed, Jack, touched to huskiness, looking after him, said :—

" A sweet land, Mate, a sweet land."

And now our green gloom purples into twilight where we have lain upon the greensward the long afternoon ; and twice my companion has hinted at a dip before dinner. To him I have read from my chronicle, and he comments something as follows :—

" You'll have to blue-pencil a lot of the stuff about me. You *do* ' get ' me somehow, and I like what you have written. But they'll make fun of you, my dear, and hurt your feelings. Listen to your father, now. I'm telling you ! "

This is considered as it deserves. But I shake my head to him, and say :—

" No. I don't believe they will."

Wednesday, May 22, 1907.

Too bright and warm the morning to stay asleep, even in this arboreal spot, we rose at six. Another and earlier riser played his part in the disturbance of rest—the saucy mynah bird, whose matin racket is full as soothing as that of our cheerfully impudent blue-jay in the Valley of the Moon. " False " mynah though he is said to be, there is nothing false about either his voice or his manners, both of which are plainly real and sincere in their abandon. Imported from India, to feed on the cutworm of a certain moth, he has made himself more familiarly at home than any other introduced bird, and

has been known to pronounce words. He is a
sagacious-looking and interesting rowdy; but
could one have choice in feathered alarm clocks,
the silver-throated skylark, another importation
to Hawaii, would come first.

But who should complain? We had not
stirred for nine solid, dreamless hours—speaking
for myself, for Jack always dreams, and vividly.
Nine hours, for either of us, is phenomenal, for
I am more or less of what he calls an " insom-
niast," and he seems to be one of those rare
individuals who thrive on short sleep. Indeed,
before our lives came together, he had for years
resolutely held to as brief hours as four and five ;
but even he was ripe to confess that this might
prove destructive to the nerves, and since then
he allows himself a sliding scale which, in the long
run, averages well—some nights three hours,
some seven, some five or six, and, but very seldom,
a night like this last. He warns that he will
put on a large waist measure ; but I am not to be
frightened. At the worst I would rather see his
splendid body fat and long-lived than his eyes
hollow, and his fine nerves on edge. Oh, he is
not a " nervous " person, despite high-strung
sensibilities. Rarely does he show his keen
tension in any fussiness of thought or speech or
action. Nevertheless, he has come to value a
measure of relaxation, as have I ; for it is a
tense, vivid life we lead in our happy hunt for
adventure ; meanwhile we work for the feeding
and housing of more than a few—to say nothing

of the up-keep of Jack's beauty-ranch in the Valley of the Moon.

Our rising young author, in search for an ideal workroom, pounced upon a shaded, wafty space out of doors, mountainward of the bungalow. Tochigi found a small table, and a box-stool for that left foot which always seeks for a rest when said author settles to writing. A larger box serves to hold extra " tools of trade," such as books and notes. Each morning, at home or abroad, Tochigi sharpens a half-dozen or more long yellow pencils with rubber tips, and dusts the table, but must never disturb the orderly litter of note-pads, scribbled and otherwise.

Within a couple of brisk hours, under my direction the boy finished the work of settling, not the least item being the installing of our big Victor and some three hundred disks ; then nothing would do but Jack must have me whirring off Wagnerian overtures and other orchestral " numbers " while I pattered about in Japanese sandals.

The typewriter shares with the " music-box " a long table in the narrow front room. Never anywhere are we quite at home until this indispensable factor of our business, with its accessories, is placed where I may conveniently copy Jack's manuscript or notes, or take his letter dictations. Since his office is under his hat, mine must be on a table large enough to support the old Remington.

By nine, with a big palm fan I was joining Jack

in the hammock where he hung between two huge algarobas, surrounded by a batch of periodicals forwarded from the coast, and we felicitated ourselves upon having risen in the comparative cool of the morning and done the more active part of the day's work. Owing to a stoppage of the blessed Trades, the air was enervatingly heavy. For the past month Hawaii has known the same unusual atmospheric conditions that marked our passage. Only a mild south wind blows—the Kona, " the sick wind," and it does seem to draw the life out of one. We are warned that when a Kona really takes charge, all things that float must look lively. Because this is not the regular season for Konas, old sea-dogs are wagging their heads.

" Do you know what you are ? " I quizzed Jack, having beaten him by a word or two in the race for knowledge.

" No, I don't. And I don't care. But do *you* know *where* you are ? " he countered.

" No, *I* don't. *You* are a *malihini*—did you know that ? "

" No, and I don't know it now. What is it ? "

" It's a newcomer, a tenderfoot, a wayfarer on the shores of chance, a——"

" I like it—it's a beautiful word," Jack curbed my literary output. " And I can't help being it, anyway. But what shall I be if I stay here long enough ? "

Recourse to a scratch-pad in my pocket divulged

the fascinating sobriquet that even an outlander, be he the right kind of outlander, might come in time—a long time—to deserve. It is *kamaai'-na*, and its significance is that of old-timer, and more, much more. It means one who *belongs*, who has come to belong in the heart and life and soil of Hawaii ; as one might say, a sub-tropical " sour-dough."

" How should it be pronounced, since you know so much ? "

" Kah-mah-ah-ee-nah," I struggled with careful notes and tongue. " But when Miss Frances says it quickly, it seems to run into ' Kah-mah-*I'*-nah.' And you mustn't say ' Kammy-hammy-hah ' for ' Kam-may-hah-may'-hah,' " I got back at him, for Kaméhaméha the Great's name had tripped us both in the books read aloud at sea.

" I'd rather be called (' *kamaaina* ') than any name in the world, I think," he deliberately ignored my efforts at his education. " I love the land and I love the people."

For be it known this is not his first sight of these islands. Eleven or twelve years ago, on the way to the sealing grounds off the Japan coast in the *Sophie Sutherland*, he first saw the loom of the southernmost of the group, Hawaii, on its side Kilauea's pillar of smoke by day and fiery glow by night. In January of 1904, bound for Korea, as correspondent to the Japanese-Russian War, he was in Honolulu for the short stop-over of the *Manchuria*, and spent as brief a time there on his return aboard the *Korea* six months later. And ever since, despite the scantiness of acquaintance, he has been drawn to return—so irresistibly as now to make a very round-about voyage to the Marquesas in the South Pacific, in order that Hawaii might be the first port of call. Often have his friends in California heard him tell of the wonderful times in Honolulu on those two flying visits, and of how good to him was " Jack " Atkinson, then Acting Governor of the Territory.

" Mate, here's something I didn't show you in the mail," Jack said presently, picking up a thick envelope addressed in his Californian agent's hand. It contained a sheaf of rejections of *The Iron Heel*, which has proved too radical for the editors, or at least for their owners' policies. " It's been turned down now by every big magazine in the United States," he went on a trifle wistfully. " I had hoped it was *timely*, and would prove a ten-strike ; but it seems I was wrong. Do you realize this means the clean loss of five or six thousand dollars ?—some pinch just now, with all this *Snark* expense of repairs, and salaries both here and at home." He lay awhile, looking up into the green lace of the algarobas. " Darn them all—they think the stuff is an attempt on my part to prophesy. It isn't. *I* don't think the worst of these things are going to happen. I wrote, as you know, merely as a warning—a warning of what might happen if the proletariat weaken in their fight

and allow the enemy to make terms with them."
Before dismissing the entire matter until the
day when he should answer the mail, he concluded :—

" They're all afraid of it, Mate-Woman. They
see their subscriptions dropping off if they run
it ; but they give hell to us poor devils of writers
if they catch us writing for the mere sake of
money instead of pure literature. What's a
fellow to do ? We've got to eat, and our families
have got to eat. And we've got to buy *holo*—
what do you call those flowy white things ? for
small wives—and sail-boats, and gather fresh
material for more stories that will and won't
sell . . ." he trailed off lugubriously.

Thus Jack on his unsuccessful and very expensive novel. Whereupon he shrugs his wide
shoulders under the blue kimono, girds the white
obi a little more snugly, picks up a note-pad
and long sharp pencil, and makes notes for a
Klondyke yarn on which he has been working,
To Build a Fire. This, being staged in the
Frozen North, is bound to captivate editors and
public alike, both of whom, mole-minded as
ever, think every other subject but the Klondyke
out of his " sphere." *He* is the timely one ;
the masses are ever lagging behind these shining
old-young thinkers. And I catch myself holding
back tears of disappointment in his disappointment, and hoping he knows the half of how sorry
I am. When I turn to look at him again, he is
shaking uncontrollably in a fit of giggles over a

cartoon in *Life*. Was there ever such a boy-man !

Although well-nigh demoralized on the voyage, due to hopeless seasickness and an equally hopeless disciplinary laxness aboard, Tochigi is rapidly regaining his old cheerful executiveness. We have had a good talk, for I have learned the value of once in a while holding friendly meetings with the servants when readjustments are to be made. Dissatisfied helpers are the doom of domestic happiness. Not all of the visitors at the Ranch have agreed with our refusal to allow any tipping. It has always seemed to us an offence to the sacred spirit of hospitality. " I pay my servants high wages to make my house a home, not a hotel. My guests are my guests in every sense. I do not want my servants to be paid for the hospitality of my house." The result has been a pleasant relation between our friends and our Japanese, who have entered wholly into the idea that they are truly sharers in the entertainment. Indeed, some sweetly amusing tales have come back from those whom we neglected to warn, of certain proud explanations that accompanied the declining of monetary favours. Of course, we do not carry this ethic beyond our own gates, wherever they may be ; it would not be fair.

Tochigi, once this simple household system is under way, will find ample time for recreation and study. Being as he is a personal servant, he will go with us on many trips and see the land-aspect of our wanderings. My work with Jack is of a nature that makes it necessary that I must be freed of a woman's usual tasks of mending, darning, brushing, packing, to say nothing of routine house duties.

"I don't want 'My Woman' to work like a horse," I remember Jack once saying, long before our marriage. "But I want her to be capable of working like a horse if it's necessary."

I like that. Every normal human being must surely feel pleasure in the ability to be "right there" in emergency—which is what Jack meant, of course. For instance, *my* "emergency" was quite unavoidable the first day ashore, when Tochigi forgot his. Also, that same night when the centipede had to be dealt with. (Jack has more than once hinted that I am ruining my best adjectives for use on *real* emergencies).

Perspiring this afternoon even in the thick shade of the great gnarled algarobas, we watched the "dear old tub" swirl on her chain-cable in stiff little squalls, and noted with satisfaction that her anchors seem to have taken good hold despite the reputed "skaty" bottom of this part of the harbour. Although in bad weather we should be obliged to move her to better shelter on the other side of the peninsula, just now we want her near ; otherwise it would mean a trudge of a mile to keep track of the repair work. And we both dislike walking.

After the warm exertion of a vociferous rubber of cribbage, which I lost, the crisp sage-green wavelets on the pink reef invited us to come out and play. So fine was the water that, once at the outer edge of the reef, I decided to venture a swim the like of which I had never known, either in length or roughness, for all my aquatic experience has been either in still creek-pools or city tanks. Not that it was actually rough ; but the snappy little staccato seas slapping my face robbed me of breath and confidence of ever reaching the yacht, at a point when she was nearer than was the jetty. The various strokes I had learned availed nothing, and I was timid of floating lest I be smothered by water washing over my upturned face. In brief, I was " in a bad way." Quietly, reassuringly, Jack spoke to me every moment, meanwhile hailing the *Snark* for a boat. He told me not to struggle, and to rest a hand on his shoulder, while he swam slowly toward the boat. Gasping and spluttering, but reassured by his calm as well as his support, by the time the lifeboat came up I was so far recovered that I merely used it for a tow to the yacht, where we rested for the return swim, on which Jack insisted that the boat escort us.

Martin, who vanished Honolulu-ward yesterday, returned this morning laden with an assortment of produce—all he could carry. His ambition was to be photographed rampant in the midst of tropical plenty, for the wonder and envy of his Kansan acquaintance. The fruity properties for the tender scene cost him all of five dollars. A mainlander might naturally conjecture Hawaii to be a land of almost automatic abundance ; but the price Martin paid is illustration of the not economical cost of living. Meat is very high, and even fish, as this morning when Tochigi had to pay twenty-five cents for three small mullet, Hawaii's best " meat that swims " (that is Jack's), peddled by a Chinese fisherman. And everything else is in proportion.

Unfortunately for our purse, the papaia on our trees is not yet ripe. Jack is wild about this fruit, and has it for every breakfast. I like it, too, but not so well as he. I think the larger part of my pleasure is in looking at it, especially on its tree, which is too artificially beautiful to seem a live and growing plant. The trunks of ours are six or seven inches in diameter, rise perfectly straight without a branch nearly to the top, where the fruit clusters thick and close around the carven bole, for so the ash-coloured wood appears with its indented markings. Among the " melons " and above them are very soft large palmated leaves, some close to the trunk and some on slender stems. And then there are the blossoms, on the axils of the leaves, twisting and twining where the fruit comes later, the little flowerets not unlike orange blossoms in appearance and odour. The trunk is said to be hollow, and there are male and female trees, which should be planted in company to ensure a good yield—for both share in bearing. The young trees are not so tall but I can easily reach the fruit ; but the trees at Miss Johnson's call for a step-ladder, or stout hands and knees for climbing. Papaia faintly resembles canteloupe and musk-melon, although more evenly surfaced ; and it tastes—what does it taste like ? We have about decided upon " sublimated pumpkin, very sublimated, but sweeter." For the table it is cut in half, length-wise, and its large canary-yellow interior scraped of a fibrous lining and a handful of slippery black seeds coated with a sort of mucus, that look for all the world like caviare, and then set in the ice-box before serving with lemon. In conjunction with beauty and palatableness, the papaia has strong peptonic virtues, and some one told us it would disintegrate a raw beefsteak over-night.

Never have we read nor heard any adequate description of the papaia tree itself ; but for sheer beauty, in an artificial sense, it is the most remark-able tree we have ever seen.

So Martin had us " snap " him, properly alert amidst his Pacific plenitude, banked under an algaroba at the water-side—coco-nuts, water-melons, pineapples, oranges, lemons, mangoes (real mangoes, but tastelessly unripe), guavas, and bananas ; not to mention papaias and taro, and a homely cabbage or two for charm against nostalgia. After which nothing would do for him but he must pose Jack and myself, and I can only hope I did not look as silly as I felt. It was all good fun, however, and Martin can now be heard developing his films in our bath-

room, his principle noise a protest at the warmth
of the " cold " water.

Beginning to wonder why Tochigi was so late
putting the breakfast dishes on the end of the
long table that holds the two machines, our surprise was delightful when with a flush on his
cheeks he led us out to where he had set a little
table under the still trees, strewn it with single
red hibiscus and glossy coral peppers from a low
hedge that trims the base of the cottage, and
served a faultless meal of papaia, shirred eggs,
a curled shaving of bacon, and fresh-buttered
toast, with perfect coffee brewed in the *Snark's*
percolator. He often arranges patterns on the
tablecloth, never two alike, from flowers or even
simple grasses and leaves—a dainty art learnt
at night-school in Japan.

Breakfast over, for an hour we lingered at
table reading aloud snatches of books on Hawaii,
and laughing over some of the freaks of her
mythology, which are not in the main so dissimilar
from those of other races, including the white, as
entirely to justify our superior mirth.

All the time I am conscious of a desire to share,
with any who may read this diary, the loveliness
of this smiling garden so green, and so sweet-
scented when little winds wake the acacia-laces
of the algarobas overhead ; where nothing really

exists beyond the red wicket, but dreams may be dreamed of mirage-like mountains shimmering in the tropic airs across the fairy lagoon.

Strolling to the bank, we sit in the long grass with our feet over the edge, and lazily watch some native women—the first we have seen—up to their ample waists, with holokus tucked high, wading slowly in the reef-shallows. One carries a small box with glass bottom, now and again she bobs out of sight under water with the box, and then comes up laughing and flinging back her dark hair that waves and ringlets in the sun. They are hunting crabs and other toothsome sea-food, which they snare in small hooped nets with handles ; and their mellow contralto voices strike the heavy air like full-throated bells, as they gossip and gurgle or break into barbaric measures of melody. Whether it be hymn or native song, the voices are musically barbaric just the same. Upon discovery of us, a truly feminine flurry of bashfulness overcomes them, but they smile like children when we call " Aloha ! " and repeat the sweet greeting softly. The mirage effect of the scene is furthered by a motionless reflection of the yacht in the glassy water, as well as of the far shore and billowy reaches of snow-white cloud. The very thought of work is shocking in such drowsy unreality of air and water and earth. Poor Jack groans over self-discipline, and there is a lag in his light and merry foot as he finally makes for the little work-table, brushes off a brown-pod and freshly dropped lace-pattern

from the algaroba, and dives into the completion
of *To Build a Fire*.

Before we were through the forenoon's business,
he creating, I transcribing, there came stepping
across the soundless lawn two dapper Japanese
gentlemen, one, the Secretary of the Japanese
Y.M.C.A. of Honolulu, the other a reporter on
the *Hawaii Shinpo*. After a ceremonial short
interview, the Secretary, with many little bows
and apologies, wanted to know if Mr. Jack London
would obligingly consent to make him the proud
possessor of " a sheet of document." Bless our
souls, what was that ? Tochigi saved further
embarrassment by explaining that his country-
man desired a page of original manuscript.

" I can't—I'm sorry ; they all belong to Mrs.
London," Jack passed him on to me.

Since all of his manuscripts have been my
most treasured property these three years, I
compromised with a " sentiment and signature,"
which Mr. Secretary had the pleasure of seeing
Jack write on the spot, and then departed with
seeming elation.

We have rounded the day with a triumphal
if slow swim to the yacht, and Jack is strutting
with pride because I made it out and back, and
even dived under the copper keel, without
assistance other than his occasional advice,
relaxing body and mind to float and rest whenever
I grew tired.

Saturday, May 25, 1907.

Observing those native women (*wahines*— wah-hee-nays) harvest crabs gave me an idea. Stirring betimes, virtuously I gathered a novel breakfast for my good man. In other words, I set baited lines along the jetty, and was soon easily netting the diminutive shellfish that hurried to the raw meat. Albert Waterhouse had furnished the method and the net, when he and Mrs. Albert dropped in last evening. No hooks are used ; the crab furnishes his own hooks, and being a creature of one idea, forgets to let go his juicy prize when the string begins to pull, so that by the time he does relinquish hold, the net is ready for his squirming fall. Although small, these yellowish-grey red-spotted crabs are spicily worth the trouble of picking to pieces. Jack, however, does not think any food is worth " wasting that much time " on, when he might be using one hand to hold a book. But he was quite enthusiastic over the plateful of picked tidbits set before him.

Here is a peculiar thing : the fish of Pearl Lochs seldom bite, and must either be netted, or speared native fashion. To be sure, there are the ancient fish-ponds, where it would be easy to use a seine ; but these ponds are closely protected by their owners, and no uncertain penalties are exacted for poaching. There are no privileges connected with the long pond that flanks our boundary to the north, so we must depend upon the unromantic peddler for our sea-fruit.

No lingering could we allow ourselves at table this morning, for we were bound Honolulu-ward on the forenoon train, to bring back the horses. " Wish I had a million dollars, so I could really enjoy life here," yawned Jack, arms above head and bare feet in the warm wet grass—it had rained heavily over-night—as he moved toward his work, with a longing eye hammock-ward to the unread magazines and files of newspapers.

Always have I remembered, in school days at Mills College, where I met and loved my first Hawaiian girl, the enthusiasm of Mrs. Susan L. Mills over the cross-saddle horse-craft of women in Honolulu, where she and her husband founded a school in early days.   So I do not now hesitate to ride my Australian saddle here.

And so, trousered, divided-skirted, booted, and spurred, both of us coatless, as the day promised to be sultry, we walked to Tony's little dummy train, on which, with fellow passengers of every yellow and brown nationality except the Hawaiian, we travelled to the very Japanesque-Americanesque village of Pearl City, where the ten o'clock through-train picked us up.   During the half-hour ride, we enjoyed the shining landscape of cane and terraced rice, long rolling hills, and the alluring purple gorges and blue valleys of the mountains to our left.   The volcanic red of the turned fields is like ours in Sonoma County, with here and there splashes of more violent madder than any at home.

I had expected Oahu to be more tropical than

this, palmy and jungly. But I woefully lacked
information, and my disappointment is nobody's
fault but my own. Even the coco-nut palms of
Hawaii are not indigenous, nor yet the bananas,
breadfruit, taro, oranges, sugar-cane, mangoes—
indeed, the fertile group does not lie in the path of
seed-carrying birds, and it remained for early
native geniuses navigating their great canoes by
the stars, and white discoverers like Cook and
Vancouver, to introduce a large proportion of
the trees and plants that look like weeds to the
sympathetic soil.

Of all imported trees, the algaroba (*Keawe*—
Kay-ah'-vay) has been the best " vegetable
missionary " to the waiting territory, and flourishes
better here than in its own countries, which seem
to include the West Indies, the southern United
States, and portions of South America. One
writer fares farther, and claims that it is the
Al-Korab, the husks of which the Prodigal Son
fed to the swine he tended. The first seed of the
algaroba was brought to Hawaii from France
by Father Bachelot, founder of the Catholic
Mission, and was planted by him in Honolulu, on
Fort Street, near Beretania, the inscription giving
the date as 1837. But an old journal of Brother
Melchoir places the date as early as 1828. This
tree is still alive and responsible for above 60,000
acres of algaroba growth in Hawaii. A busy
tree these seventy-odd years ! Left to itself, the
algaroba seems to prefer an arid and stony bed,
judging from the manner in which it had reclaimed

and forested the reefy coast about Honolulu, which was formerly a bare waste. On this island, as well as on Molokai and Hawaii, it has changed large tracks of rocky desert into abundantly wooded lands.

Speeding along, we noticed a number of the exotic monkey-pod trees. The tropical American name is *samang*, though sometimes it is called the rain-tree, from its custom of blossoming at the beginning of the rainy season. It is broad-spreading, flat-topped, with enormous trunk, and like the algaroba is a member of the acacia family, folding its feathery leaves at night. It is wonderfully ornamental for large spaces, but cannot be used to shade streets, as its quick growth plays ludicrous havoc with side-walks and gutters. I have read that a common sight in the islands is a noonday monkey-pod shade of 150 feet diameter.

" The Japanese city of Honolulu ! " burst from my astonished lips, once we were out of the station and walking toward the far-famed fish market. For the Japanese are in full possession of block after block of tenements, stores, and eating-places that fairly overlap one another, while both men and women go about their business in the national garb of kimono and sandals.

The market was more or less depleted of the beautiful coloured fish Jack had been so anxious for me to see, and we plan to come back some time in the early morning, at which time both the fish and the quaint crowd are at their best.

Not until in the business centre of the city proper were our eyes gladdened by the sight of our own kind and the native Hawaiians themselves, although the latter have become so intermixed with foreign strains that comparatively few in Honolulu can be vouched for as pure bred. According to the latest census, there are less than 30,000 all-Hawaiians in Hawaii Nei, with nearly 8,000 *hapa-hooles* (hah-pah-hah-o-lays—quickly, hah-pah-how-lees), which means half-whites.   The total population of Honolulu is around the 40,000 mark, and of these roughly 10,000 only are white.

I do not often form expectations in a way that lays me open to serious disillusionment.   But I had certainly pictured Honolulu differently ; and the abrupt evidence of my eyes was a trifle saddening.   The name Honolulu is said to mean " the sheltered," and it would not inaptly refer to the population of far-drifted nationalities that shelters in its sweetly hospitable confines.

Soon, however, all temporary dash to hopes of beholding a Hawaiian city became absorbed in the types that had given rise to disappointment, and in the unfolding of the quaint town itself, with its bright shop-windows, and sidewalks where real, unmistakably real Hawaiian wahines sat amidst a riot of flowers for sale, themselves crowned with *leis* (lay'-ees-wreaths), and offering others to passers.   Besides, something happened that awoke in me a revolutionizing emotion, or concept, or whatever it may be called, that I had never known of myself, nor been brought up to consider. Born and reared in the ultimate West, where the negro problem troubleth not, the darky gardener (who was half-Cherokee Indian), to say nothing of the vegetable and wash-Chinaman, honest as the long day, were my childhood friends, conspicuously generous and benevolent on Oriental holidays. This emotion, or concept, it would seem was born of the instant need, as probably vital concepts are most often brought into being. And it shook me to the foundations. Do not confuse this with race *hatred*. My respect and admiration for Japan are profound. It is a different thing altogether. And this was the way of it :—

Mr. Rowell and Jack were walking together, talking busily, and I had wandered well ahead on the narrow sidewalk of the winding lane, where blossoming trees hung over old walls and fences, and there was barely room for vehicles to pass. I was dreaming along, when suddenly I found myself confronted by a bristle-headed, impudent-eyed Japanese coolie who had stepped out from a doorway close to the pavement. Even at my leisurely pace it would have been only seconds when I should have come up to him, and, for one of those seconds, it looked as though he were not going to give room. Without consciously reasoning I knew that I, a white woman, should rather have died than step around this coolie Asiatic. In his own country—perhaps ; in mine, or any other than his, decidedly no. For an instant I was " seeing red," and when I briefly " came to,'' my hands were fists, and I felt as if the Jap's last-instant side-step into his doorway had saved me from an exhibition of the boxing tactics Jack has taught me.   Even then I came within a wise ace of slapping the insolent grin my furious side-glance did not miss.   I can only hope I looked more pugilistic than a slap.   This man, like many others we saw to-day, is of totally different breed from the familiar Japanese in the cities of Cali-fornia—the refined, student house-boys like our Tochigi of the gentle voice and unfailing courtesy. These coolies are of bigger, sturdier frame and coarser features, with a masculine, aggressive expression in their darker skinned faces.   Jack's practised eye leads him to think that a larger proportion of them is from the rank and file that served in the Japanese-Russian War three years ago.   He watched me rather curiously the while I was telling him the incident at lunch, and I knew I was flushing to the memory of my racial upset, when he said, " Why, the poor kid ! She's learning the world ! " But he made no further comment.   Neither he nor Mr. Rowell had observed the quiet happening, and " mad " though I was at the time, I cooled down almost immediately, and soon forgot everything in a comical experience we all three shared when we tried to lunch in the Alexander Young Hotel— a modest sky-scraper of grey stone, at the top of which a café is conducted.   Thither we repaired, and, it being a good half-hour before noon, when we stepped out of the elevator, a flaxen-haired woman behind the cashier's desk was the only person visible. In lack of steward or waiter, Jack led the length of the cool room to a table in a windowed corner where we could look over the city. Here an angle in the room brought us to the notice of a waiter who lost no time in whispering over Jack's white-shirted shoulder to the effect that no gentlemen without coats were admitted to the ·chaste precincts of the café! I was alert to hear Jack ask him for the loan of a coat, as he had done one sparkling early morning at the Titchfield in Port Antonio, Jamaica, when we went for breakfast before starting on a two-days' horseback trip across the mountains to Kingston. Oh, indeed, and Jack did not fail to ask this Honolulu waiter for the coat ; and the man was so embarrassed that he compromised with his own dignity by suggesting that he place us at a little less conspicuous table, some twenty feet nearer the elevator. We did not exactly see how it was less conspicuous, and I looked for Jack to demur on principle ; but for once he was more interested in luncheon than quizzing the waiter. Furthermore, we had a guest ; and the guest already had raised Jack's appetite for an alligator-pear " cocktail "—a relish made of the pear cut in cubes and seasoned in catsup and lemon and salt.

I am .sure the fair-tressed cashier, with her desk telephone, was the guilty one, for presently the brassy elevator commenced to deliver a steady stream of Honolulans, each unit of which addressed her and then followed her nod towards our " less conspicuous table." Jack, as an old Irishwoman once told him, looks more like his photographs than they look like him, and is often recognized by strangers who have only seen his face in the newspapers ; so there was no taking of Mr. Rowell by mistake, or of any one else in the rapidly filling tables, and I think the management should be grateful for the unwonted early-luncheon crowd Jack so innocently drew. The steward, who had until now worn an exceedingly detached expression, waxed assiduous in suggestions for a true Honolulu repast. With a grin and a " what's the use anyway ! " Jack let him order for us at his own sweet will. I have to thank him for introducing me to guava ice-cream, the deliciously flavoured crushed fruit staining the cream salmon-pink. Jack's final comment about the affair was :—

" Well, I leave it to any one if it isn't silly that in a tropic city, like Honolulu, the conventions of altogether different climates should make slaves of men ! "

On the streets many go about in the ordinary business suits of the mainland ; but, thank goodness, all are not so foolish. At least, thank goodness, that *we* don't have to follow their example, but may happily be counted with the " white-robed ones " who compose the fitting majority.

Pasadena, with all its riot of roses, is not more

beautiful than lovely Honolulu glowing with wonderful flowering vines as well as large trees that vie with the vines in gorgeousness of blossom. And Honolulu has her own roses as well.

Inside Mr. Rowell's gate I sat me down, breathless with the astounding mantle of colour that lay over house and barns and fence. I had heard carelessly of the poinciana regia, and bougainvillea, and golden shower, and was already familiar with the single red and pink hibiscus, which won my affection in the West Indies. And again I must register complaint that either the globe-trotters we have met have short memories or little care for these things, for we were quite unprepared for the splendour of them.

" There ain't no such tree," Jack broke our silence before the poinciana regia, the " flame tree," and *flamboyante* of the French. It was named in honour ("Some honour," Jack observed) of Poinci, Governor-General of the West Indies around the middle of the seventeenth century, who wrote upon their natural history. I have never seen anything so spectacular growing out of the ground. It might have been manufactured in Japan—like the papaia—for stage property. The smooth grey trunk expands at the base into a buttress-like formation that corresponds to the principal roots, with an effect on the eye of an artificial base broad enough to support the grey pillar without underpinning. The tree grows flat-topped, not unlike the monkey-pod, and the foliage of fine pinnate leaves, lying

horizontally layer upon layer, carries out the
" made in the Orient " illusion. But the wonder
of wonders is the burst of flaming bloom covering
all the green with palpitating scarlet. Clearly
red in the flowering mass, it is another marvel to
examine the separate blossoms, one of which
covered the palm of my hand. How can one
describe it ! In form it was more suggestive of
an orchid than anything I could think of, and
there were one or two small, salmon-yellow petals.
The petals were soft and crinkly as those of a
Shirley poppy, fine and delicate fairy crêpe.

Under this gorgeous shelter Mr. Rowell raises
orchids for the market, and I thought I never
could tear myself from the lovely butterfly things.
I was sorry I could not carry on horseback the
ones so freely offered.

In the rambling garden one could but turn
from one bursting wonder to another. The most
ramshackle house, chicken-coop, fence, or barn,
is glorified by the bougainvillea vine, named
after the early French navigator. In colour a
bright yet soft brick-red, or terra-cotta, like old
Spanish tiling, it flows over everything it touches,
sending showers and rockets that softly pile in
masses on roof and arbour. Close to the flowers,
I discovered they were not exactly flowers, these
painted petals, but more of the order of leaves
or half-formed petals. It is the bracts themselves,
which surround the very inconspicuous blossoms,
that hold the colour—as with the poinsettia. We
had already noticed, in other gardens, great

masses of magenta vine, which Mr. Rowell told us is also bougainvillea, and is of two varieties, one a steady bloomer, season upon season. There are other colours, too—salmon-pink, orange, and scarlet. And speaking of the poinsettia, which even in California we cherish in pots, here in magical Hawaii it grows out of doors, sometimes to a height of fifteen or twenty feet —as do begonias on some of the islands ; but I, for one, want to see to believe !

We are willing to believe anything about the guava, be it tree or shrub, and it is both in this sunset land, for to-day we feasted on its yellow globes—dozens of them. Ripe, they were better far than the ice-cream, with soft edible rind enclosing a heart of pulpy seeds crushed-strawberry in tint, which, oddly enough, taste not unlike strawberries—stewed strawberries with a dash of lemon. Before I realize it, I am breaking that vow not to try describing the taste of foreign fruits.

At length we must tear rudely from this Edenic enclosure, and saddle the little bay mares, It was good to feel the creaking leather and the eager pull on bits, although in the case of Jack's mount, Koali (Morning Glory), that eager pull was all in a retrograde direction when he attempted to leave town. City limits were good enough for the Morning Glory, and her rider had a perilous time on the slippery creature, who had evidently been not too well broken. My heart was in my mouth at her narrow escapes from electric cars, and from sliding falls on the tracks. Finally she capitulated, and all went smoothly once we struck the fine stretch of road to the peninsula, which leads through the famous Damon gardens that are like an enchanted wood. This is the way to travel, intimately in touch with the lovely land and sea and sky, without having to crane our necks out of car windows or after vanishing views on the wrong side of the coach. For the most part we went slowly, as the horses were soft, and found it very warm, with that heavy, moist, perfumed air that more than all the scenery makes one feel the strangeness of a new country. Tall sugar-cane rustled in the late fan of wind, and a sudden brief shower, warm as milk, wet our coatless shoulders. Little fear of catching cold from a drenching in this climate where it is always summer.

The owner of the mares assures us that all they need be fed is the sorghum that grows outside our fence along the roadway, balanced by a measure of grain twice daily. We are also at liberty to pasture them in a handy vacant lot, and Tochigi will feed the grain which he has stored in the tiny servant-house where he sleeps.

" They're used to out-doors day and night, so the sky is sufficient stable-roof," Mr. Rowell praised the climate. And so, our possession of the horses is all pleasure and slight responsibility.

Little as I really saw of Honolulu on this flying trip, enough it was to fill my head to overflowing with pictures ; while that resplendent garden of *flamboyante* and bougainvillea and orchids and golden guavas stays with me like a dream.

PEARL HARBBOUR,
Tuesday, May 28, 1907.

One old-time sojourner on this coral strand fitly wrote : " When all days are alike, there is no reason for doing a thing to-day rather than to-morrow." Whether or not he lived up to his wise conclusion I do not know ; but the average hustling white-skin, filled with unreasonable ambition to visit other shores, does not live up, or down, to any such maxim. Maybe it is a mistake ; maybe we should pay more heed to the lure of *dolce far niente.* Even so, for us it is not expedient, and we may as well forget it. Jack does not regard it seriously, anyway. His deep-chested vitality and personal optimism, together with his gift of the gods, sleep under any or all conditions, if he but will to sleep, quite naturally render him intolerant of coddling himself in any climate under the sun, no matter how inimical to his supersensitive white skin. And I decline to worry. It is so easy to acquire the habit of worrying about one's nearest and dearest, to the ruin of all balance of true values. Nothing annoys and antagonizes Jack so much as inquiries about his feelings when he himself has not given them a thought. Time enough when the thing happens,

is his practice, if not his theory ; but in justice
I must say that he applies this unpreparedness
only to himself, and has ever a shrewd and
scientific eye for the welfare of those dependent
upon him, although never will he permit himself
to " nag." " I'm telling you, my dear," once,
twice, possibly thrice—and there's an end on't.

Everything is freshening in the cool trade-wind
that is commencing to wave the live-palm-leaf
fans, and on the slate-blue horizon soft masses
of low trade-wind clouds pile and puff and promise
refreshment—" wool-packs," sailors call them,
which " listens rather too warm," as Albert
Waterhouse would say. The past few days of
variable weather have roasted us one minute,
and steamed us the next when the uncooling
rains descended. But it is all in the tropic
pattern, and it is nice never to require anything
heavier than summer " pretties," as Jack loves
to name them.

" Now, don't stint yourself, whatever you do,
Mate," he urged this morning, half-apprehensive
lest I do so in face of the " Iron Heel " disaster.
" Get a lot of things—lots of those loose ruffly
things—and some evening dresses.   You'll need
evening things when we go up to stay in Honolulu "

" Hello, Twin Brother ! " he greeted me yesterday, when booted and trousered, I was bridling
Lehua. " I wish you didn t have to put on the
skirt, you look so eminently smart and appropriate ! "

" Be patient," I told him.   " We'll all be riding

this way in a few years, see if we aren't. You wait."

But the cheery prophecy of public good sense could not stifle a sigh as I added to the natty boyish togs the long, hot black skirt. What a silliness to put the " weaker sex " to such disadvantages—as if we did not manifest our bonny brawn by surviving to fight them !

To the village we galloped to have Koali and Lehua shod at the blacksmith's, and odd enough it was to see a Japanese working on their hoofs, for somehow one does not readily associate the thought of horses with the Japanese. This one did a fair piece of business, however. But for a succession of violent downpours, we should have taken a long ride. There is inexpressible glory in this broken weather ; one minute you move in a blue gloom under a low-hanging sky, and the next, all brilliance of heaven bursts through, gilding and bejewelling the vivid-green world.

This date marks a vital readjustment in ship matters. Two of the *Snark's* complement are to return to the mainland, and Jack has cabled to Gene to come down by first steamer and take hold of the engines. Not to mention many other details of incomprehensible neglect aboard by the undisciplinary sailing-master, the costly sails have been left to mildew in their tight canvas covers on the booms in all this damp weather, with deck-awnings stretched *under* the booms instead of protectingly above. And no bucket of water has been sluiced over the deck since our arrival eight days ago, necessitating the not inconsiderable expense of recalking thus early in the voyage. The appearance of the deck can be guessed ; and otherwise no effort has been put forth to bring the yacht into presentable order, nor any interest nor headwork displayed in forwarding repairs. If a salaried master will let his valuable charge lapse, there is no cure but to get one who will not. As for the machinery, Gene had begged for a chance to sail as engineer, and now that Bert has concluded that after all adventure is not what he wanted, Gene shall be given opportunity to show what he knows about gasolene.

Last Sunday we lunched with the Waterhouses and their rollicking week-end crowd from town, who showed what *they* thought of conventional restrictions in tropic cities, by spending the day in light clothing and bare feet, resting or romping over house and grounds. Mrs. Gretchen's German papa, Mr. Kopke, who is Superintendent of the Honolulu Iron Works, was also there, and came back with us to take a personal look-see at our wrecked engine. To-day he made a special trip from the city, bringing an engineer, and the upshot was a more encouraging report than Mr. Kopke had deemed possible from his first inspection. "Anyway," he cheered our dubiousness, "you're a whole lot better off than the little yacht that piled ashore on the reef outside yonder this morning." They decided that the repairing can be done aboard the *Snark* here at Pearl

Harbour, instead of our having the nuisance of taking her to Honolulu, and curtailing our time in this green refuge.

So Jack's face, that had been fairly downcast for two or three days, cleared like an Oahu sky after a thunder-shower ; and later he said to me, with a familiar little apologetic smile :—

" Mate Woman, you mustn't mind my getting a little blue sometimes. I can't help it. When a fellow does his damndest to be square with everybody, buys everything of the best in the market and makes no kick about paying for it, and then gets thrown down, the way I've been thrown down, with the whole building and running of this boat, from start to finish—why, it's enough to make him bite his veins and howl. A man picks out a clean wholesome way of making and spending his money, and every goldarned soul jumps him. If I went in for race-horses and chorus-girls and big red automobiles, there'd be no end of indulgent comment. But here I take my own wife and start out on good clean adventure —Oh, Lord ! Lord ! What's a fellow to think ? . . . Only, don't you mind if I get the blues *once* in a while. I don't very often. . . . And don't think I'm not appreciating your own cheerfulness. I don't miss a bit of it, my dear, and I love you to death for it. . . . And you and I are what count ; and we'll live our life in spite of them."

Other people have their troubles, too. Bert,

for instance, who is the recipient of much gratuit-
ous sympathy from all hands.   He does not think
the occasion at all funny, and one can hardly
blame him.   With blood in his eye, he is looking
for a certain reporter on one of the local sheets.
The reporter had happened upon the fact that
Bert's father, who years ago was a sheriff on
Kauai, the " Garden Island," was shot and killed
by a native leper, a wild free spirit of his race who
fled to the mountain fastnesses to escape deporta-
tion to the settlement on Molokai.   It was a
tragic episode, heaven knows ; but the bright
young reporter, who cannot have been long in the
islands, rendered Bert's situation quite desperate
by airily stating that Bert was the *son* of the
famous leper of Kauai !

Again referring to that beloved scrap-heap,
the *Snark*, there's à comedian in our own small
tragedy, although he doesn't know it.   His
sweet and liquid name is Schwank, assumably
Teutonic, and, with hands eloquent of bygone
belaying pins, " every finger a fish-hook, every
hair a rope-yarn," he tinkers about the boat
in the capacity of carpenter.   With his large
family, he lives on the other side of the peninsula,
and bids fair to be a great diversion to us all.
Belike he has of old been a sad swashbuckler,
for he hints at dark deeds on the high seas, of
castaways and stowaways, of smuggled opium
and other forbidden sweets ; and he gloats over
memories of gleaming handfuls of pearls exchanged
for handfuls of sugar in the goodly yesterdays.

Why did he not make it pailfuls of pearls while he was on the subject ? In my own dreams of pearl-gathering in the Paumotus and Torres Straits far to the south-west, I never allow myself to think in less measure than a lapful. But pondering upon this theatrical old pirate's vaunted exchange, I cannot help wishing I had been a sugar planter, for I care more for pearls than for sugar.

Late this afternoon we took out the horses for a few red miles over the roads of Honolulu Plantation. The rich rolling country recalled rides in Iowa, its high green cane, over our heads, rustling and waving like corn of our Middle West. And everywhere we turned were the stout and gnarly Japanese labourers, women as well as men. Female field labourers may be picturesque in some lands ; but I am blest if these tiny Japanese women, with their squat, misshapen bodies and awful bandy legs, and blank, sexless faces, look well in ours ! Their heads are bound in white cloth, while a-top, fitting as well as Happy Hooligan's crown, sit small sun-hats of coarse straw. From under bent backs men and women alike lowered at us with their slant, inscrutable eyes. Tony, who claims a smattering of their language, tells us : " I think Americans no lika-da talk those Japanese I hear on my train and Pearl City." And there are 56,000 of them by now in this covetable territory—prolific, and averse to intermarrying with any of the many other adopted bloods in Hawaii.

Sunday night, after Mr. Kopke left, we went up by train to Honolulu, to fulfil a dinner engagement with Mr. and Mrs. Charles L. Rhodes, to whom we had been introduced in the lobby of the Alexander Young the day of our " conspicuous " luncheon upstairs.   Mr. Rhodes is editor of the evening paper, *The Star*, and Mr. Walter Gifford Smith, editor of the *Pacific Commercial Advertiser*, whom Jack had met here in 1904, was also invited.   The other guests were Brigadier-General John H. Soper and his family.   It is interesting to note that General Soper is the first officer ever honoured by the Hawaiian Government—by any one of the successive Hawaiian Governments—with the rank and commission of General.   He had been in charge of the police during the unsettled days of the Revolution, and later on was made Marshal of the Republic of Hawaii, in effect previous to her annexation by the United States.

Mr. and Mrs. Rhodes live in a cosy vine-clambered cottage, set in a rosy lane tucked away behind an avenue clanking with open electric cars ; such a pretty lane, a garden in itself, closed at one end where a magnificent bougainvillea flaunts magenta banners, and a slanting coco-nut palm traces its deep-green frondage against the sky.

This was a most pleasant glimpse into a Honolulu home, and our new friends further invited us to go with them to a reception Wednesday evening.   Now, be it known that neither of us is over-fond of public receptions ; but this one is irresistible, for Prince Jonah Kuhio Kalanianaole and his royal wife are to receive in state, in their own home, with the Congressional Party now visiting the Islands from Washington, on the Reception Committee.   Also, there is a possibility that Her Majesty, Liliuokalani, the last crowned head of the fallen monarchy, may be there.   In these territorial times of Hawaii, such a gathering may not occur again, and it is none too early for us to be glad of a chance to glimpse something of what remains of the incomparably romantic monarchy that died so courageously.

Heigh-O, palm-trees and grasses !   This is a lovely world altogether, and we are most very glad to be in it.   But it has its small drawbacks, say when the honoured Chief Executive of one's own United States of America makes an error quite out of keeping with his august superiority. This placid grey-and-gold morning, arriving by first train from town, and before we had risen from our post-breakfast feast of books at the jolly little out-door table, a perfectly nice and affable young man, whose unsettled fortune—or misfortune—it is to be a newspaper reporter, invaded our vernal privacy.   In his hand no scrip he bore, but a copy of *Everybody's Magazine*, portly with advertising matter, his finger inserted at an article by Theodore Roosevelt on the subject of " nature-fakers."   In this more or less just diatribe, poor Jack London is haled forth and flayed before a deceived reading-public as one of several pernicious writers who should be restrained from misleading the adolescent of America with incorrect representation of animal life and psychology. An incident in Jack's *White Fang*, published last Fall, companion novel to *The Call of the Wild*, is selected for damning illustration of the author's infidelity to nature. Our Teddy, oracle and idol of adventurous youth, declares with characteristic emphasis that no lynx could whip a wolf-dog as Jack's lynx whipped Kiche, the wolf-dog. But the joke is on the President this time, as any one can see who will take the trouble to look up the description in *White Fang*. And lest you have no copy convenient, let me explain that Jack never said the lynx whipped the wolf-dog. Quite to the contrary :—

" Why, look here," he laughed, running his eye rapidly down the magazine column, " he says that the lynx in my story killed the wolf-dog. It did nothing of the kind. That doesn't show that Mr. Roosevelt is as careful an observer as *Everybody's* would have us believe. My story is about the wolf-dog killing the lynx—and eating it ! "

" I hope he'll get it straight," he mused, after the departing form of the reporter with a " good story." " I can see myself writing an answer to Mr. Roosevelt later on, in some magazine."

Jack's hope that his response to the charge of " nature-faking " would be honestly reported, was a reflex to the relentless treatment he has

suffered from the press of the Pacific Coast.   It
would seem as if the newspaper proprietors from
the Canadian to the Mexican borders had filed
standing orders to give him the worst of it wherever
easiest to do so, and to go out of the way to do
so whenever possible.   This is undoubtedly due
to the menace of his socialistic utterances ; but
what a distorted civilization it is that makes a
man, who has unaided fought his way up from
nether levels of circumstance, pay so bitterly
for his stark humanitarian politics.   " Lots of
the newspaper men do not dislike me, and like
my work, I know ; and I hate to see them have
to sacrifice their own convictions and consciences
to the policies of their employers—or starve.
And reporters, in common with the general run
of men, don't like to starve."

What did he himself do when he was a newspaper man ? may be asked.   The answer is, that
even when he was nearly starving, he held himself
back from the temptation to do any work for the
dailies except very occasional, special, *signed*
articles.   I look for him to begin, at the first
favourable moment, a novel that will be an
autobiography of his struggles to gain recogni-
tion.   He has often spoken of his desire to do
this.

The newspapers of Honolulu, this Farthest
West of his own country, have shown toward him
no influence of the unkindness of his home State,
but have been all that is hospitable, and this in
face of the rebuff put upon their city when we

sailed calmly by to the suburbs.   From various
sources again we hear of the welcomes that were
waiting along the wharves, the garlands that were
woven for our necks.

It must be forgiven that I jump from theme
to theme in more or less distracted manner ; for
if the way of my life is one of swift adjustments,
so must be the honest way of my chronicle.   And
so, from presidents, and reporters, wolf-dogs,
and politics, lynxes, and ethics, and histories of
author-husbands, I shift to fripperies, and gala
gardens, and Polynesian princes.

My party-gown (not a new one, for thus far I
have not obeyed the gentle mandate to " buy lots
of them ") hangs on a line across a corner of the
big room, faultlessly pressed by the æsthetic
Tochigi, with yards and yards of Spanish lace,
souvenir of Santiago de Cuba, about the shoulders
arranged with unerring taste by fair Gretchen.
It is always a pleasure to hear her benevolent
" How are you people ? " and Albert's cheery
" Zing ! " at the red gate.   Often he and the
Madonna stroll over in the dusk, in their hands
slender red-glowing punks to ward off mosquitoes
—the " undesirable immigrants " that have in-
fested Hawaii's balmy nights these eighty years,
ever since the ship *Wellington*, last from San Blas,
Mexico, unwittingly discharged them in her otherwise empty water-barrels at Lahaina, on Maui.
It was a sad exchange for unpolluted drinking
water.   Fortunately the days are free of the
pests ; but woe to the malihini who kens not

deftly how to tuck his bobinet under the edges of his mattress.

The enchantment of our lovely acre and the novel way of living, it would seem, is being challenged by the varying temptations of the Capital.   To-night we attend the reception, and to-morrow ride to Waikiki to spend a few days on the beach.

PEARL HARBOUR,
Thursday, May 30, 1907.

Jack preceded me into town to keep a business engagement with the Iron Works people, who are taking the kindest interest in the *Snark* repairs.

I took the five o'clock train to Honolulu, where Jack met me, and we drove in a funny little one-horse carriage to the "Royal Hawaiian Hotel" for dinner.   Ever since Jack's letters to me from Hawaii three years ago, I have longed to see this noted tropic hostelry with its white tiers of balconies and its Hawaiian orchestra, and the red and green lights which its foreign guests execrate and love.   Last evening, however, the hotel was quiet—no music, no coloured lights, no crowd.   But the gardens were there, and the fairy balconies, on the lowest of which we dined most excellently, with an unforeseen guest.   Before the "American-plan" dinner hour, we were sitting in a cool corner talking of our visit to the beach, when a bearded young man stepped briskly up, with :—

" You're Jack London, aren't you ?—My name is Ford."

" Oh, yes," Jack returned, quickly on his feet— " Alexander Hume Ford. I heard you were in Honolulu, and have wanted to see you. I've read lots of your stuff—and all of your dandy articles in *The Century*."

Mr. Ford could hardly spare time to look his pleasure, nor to be introduced to me, before rushing on, in a breathless way that made one wonder what was the hurry :—

" Now look here, London," in a confidential undertone. ' I've got a lot of whacking good material—for stories, you understand. *I* can't write stories—there's no use my trying. My fiction is rot—rot, I tell you. I can write travel stuff of sorts, but it takes no artist to do that. You *can* write stories—the greatest stories in the world—and I'll tell you what : I'll jot down some of the things I've got hold of here and everywhere, and you're welcome to them. . . . What d'you say ? "

Jack suggested that he join us at dinner, and he talked a steady stream all through—a mine of information about everything under the sky, it would seem, for he has travelled widely. At present he is interested in reviving the old Hawaiian sport of surf-boarding on the breakers, and promised to see us at Waikiki later on, and show us how to use a board. When he left we were able to draw the first long breath in two hours. In his atmosphere one had the sense of being *speeded up :* but his generous good-nature was worth it.

On the electric car bound for Waikiki, we found ourselves in a holiday crowd that sat and stood, or hung on the running-boards—a crowd that convinced me Honolulu was Honolulu after all. The passengers on the running-boards made merry way for the haole wahine, while a beaming Hawaiian, a gentleman if ever was one, gave me his seat, raising his garlanded hat as he did so. The people made a kaleidoscope of colour— white women in evening gowns and fluffy wraps, laughing Hawaiian and hapa-haole girls in gaudy holokus and woolly crocheted " fascinators," the native men sporting brilliant *leis* of fresh flowers, the most characteristic being the *ilima*, which, strung on thread, forms an orange-coloured inch-rope greatly affected for neck-garlands and hat-bands. Like ourselves, they were all making for the gardens of their Prince.

Some three miles from the centre of town, we alighted at the big white Moana Hotel, where, in a lofty seaward lanai, overlooking a palmy carriage-court, with her husband waited Mrs. Rhodes—a picture in the subdued light, her gown of soft white cloaked with a Chinese mandarin mantle of rose and green and gold.   Her caressing manner, and a gift of making one feel pleased with oneself, all went to perfect our first hour at Waikiki, spent in sipping from cool glasses while we rested in large rattan chairs, for none but a malihini moves quickly here.   Lovely

indeed was this first glimpse of Hawaii's cele-
brated watering-place as we lounged in the liquid
night-breeze from over rolling star-tipped waters
that broke in long white lines on the dim crescent
beach.

At length we strolled across broad Kalakaua
Avenue and into a park where great looming
trees were festooned high and low with coloured
lights—Prince Cupid's private gardens thrown
wide to his own people as well as to his foreign
guests. A prodigious buzz and hum came from
over by a lighted building, and drawing nearer
across the lawn, we stepped to the measure of a
fanfare of martial music from Berger's Royal
Hawaiian Band. From an immense open tent
where many were sitting at little tables, the lilting
of a Hawaiian orchestra of guitars and *ukuleles*
(oo-koo-lay'-lees) blended into the general festive
din ; and then, threading purely the medley of
sound, was heard a woman's voice that was like
a violin, rising high and higher, dominating the
throng until it lapsed into absolute silence. It
was the sweetest of Hawaiian singers, the famous
Madame Alapai, and a prodigious clapping and
shouting went up from all over the grounds when
she had finished, ceasing instantly at the first
crystal tone of her ready encore.

Like a child at a fair, I had no attention for the
way of my feet in the grass, and Jack laughed
paternally at my absorption as he piloted me by
the elbow, with a " Dear kid—it's a pleasure to
take you anywhere, you do have such a good time ! "

A pretty Hawaiian maid at the dressing-tent greeted us haole wahines with a smiling " Aloha," and led to where we could leave wraps, and dust noses and pat coiffures ; after which the four of us picked a way through the company of women, lovely in their trailing gowns, and men in black and white evening attire or glittering army and navy uniforms, while all around under the trees in the background hundreds of Hawaiians looked on, their dusky faces and beautiful eyes eloquent with curiosity and interest. Up a green terrace we paced, to the broad encircling lanai of what looked to be an immense grass house. And grass house it proved, in which the royal owners dwelt before the building of the more modern mansion.

This particular entertainment, including as it did the Congressional Party, was unique in its significance. To the right stood the Delegate, Prince Jonah Kuhio Kalanianaole, a well-known figure in Washington, D.C., a dark, well-featured, medium-sized man in evening dress, handsome enough, but quite eclipsed, in my eyes, by the gorgeous creature at his side, pure Hawaiian like himself, his wife, the Princess Elizabeth. The bigness of her was a trifle overwhelming to one new to the physical aristocracy of the island peoples. You would hesitate to call her fat—she is just big, sumptuous, bearing her splendid pro- portions with the remarkable poise I had already noticed in Hawaiian women, only more magni- ficently. Her bare shoulders were beautiful, the pose of her head majestic, with heavy fine dark hair that showed bronze lights in its wavy mass. She was superbly gowned in silk that had a touch of purple or lilac about it, just the tone for her full, black, calm eyes and warm tawny skin. For these of chief blood are many shades fairer than the commoners.

Jack and I, under our breath, agreed that we could not expect ever to behold a more queenly woman. My descriptive powers are exasperatingly inept to picture the manner in which this Princess stood, touching with hers the hands of all who passed before her, with a brief, graceful droop of her fine head, and a fleeting, perfunctory, yet gracious flash of little teeth under her small fine mouth. Glorious she was, the Princess Kalanianaole, every inch a princess in the very tropical essence of her. Always shall I remember her as a resplendent exotic flower, swaying and bending its head with unaffected, innate grace.

One and all they filed past, her own race, proud and humble alike, kissing the small, jewelled brown hand, while the white Americans merely touched it with their own. And what came most vividly to me, out of the conventionality, out of the scene so wrapped about with state and pomp, was a fleeting, shifting glint of the wild in her great black eyes, shining through the garmenture of her almost incredible culture and refinement —a fitful spark of the passing savage soul of her, one of a people but lately clothed in modern manners.

To the left of the deposed Princess, in a large

arm-chair, sat an even more interesting, if not so beautiful, personage—no less than Queen Liliuokalani, the last sovereign of the Kingdom of Hawaii, sister and successor to the far-famed and much-travelled King Kalakaua. The Queen is rarely on view to foreigners, especially Americans, for she loves us not, albeit her consort, Governor John Owen Dominis, dead these sixteen years, was the son of a Massachusetts captain. I was glad to be well down the line, as I had more time to watch her, for the vigour of her great fight of but yesterday to preserve the Crown of Hawaii, is to me one of the most interesting dramas in history—bleeding tragedy to her.

Photographs and paintings do not flatter Queen Liliuokalani. All I have seen depict a coarseness and heaviness that is entirely absent. I was therefore surprised, brought face to face with Her Majesty, to find that face rather thin, strong, and pervaded with an elusive refinement that might be considered her most striking characteristic, if anything elusive can be striking. But this evasive effect, in a countenance fairly European in feature, was due, I think, to the expression of the narrow black eyes, rather close-set, which were unmistakably savage in their cold hatred of everything American. And who can blame her ? As near as I can figure it, she was tricked and trapped by brains for which her brain, remarkable though it be, was no match. Imagine her emotions, she who received special favour from Queen Victoria at the Jubilee in London ;

she who then had the present Kaiser for her right-hand courtier at royal banquets, and the royal escort of Duke This and Earl That upon public occasions, now sitting uncrowned, receiving her conquerors.

It is easier for the younger ones ; but the old Queen's pretence is thin, and my sympathy, for one, is very warm toward her. There is no gain-saying that truism, " the survival of the fittest," in the far drift of the human, and the white indubitably has proved the fittest ; but our hearts are all for this poor old Queen-woman, although I could not help wondering if she would have liked us any better had she known. Most certainly, when our eyes met, in that brief look there was nothing of the tender suavity of the Hawaiian, only abyssmal dislike. Taking my cue from those preceding, I offered a dubious paw, which she touched gingerly, as if she would much prefer to slap it. It was a distinct relief to meet the prankish eye of Acting-Governor " Jack " Atkinson, my Jack's old friend (who stood next the Queen's chair, murmuring in her ear the names of strangers), and surrender my timorous hand to his hearty clasp. " How are you, old man ? " he whispered to Jack.

And thence on, down one side of the long lanai, and off to the lawn, we ran the gauntlet of a bowing, embarrassed, amused string of Con-gressmen with their wives and daughters, all smilingly uncomfortable in the absence of intro-ductions, since they formed the Reception Committee in this stranger city. We undoubtedly looked as foolish, when the tension was immeasurably let down by a jolly young Congressman who blurted out :—

"*That* Jack London ! Why didn't somebody tell us ? Great Scot ! "

A subdued titter went up, and I said to the grinning Jack : " That's how you pay for your ' Dream Harbour ' seclusion ! "

Now we were free to mingle with the charming throng, and it was " Aloha " here and " Aloha " there, lovely and all-loving salutation, employed alike by white and native. We happened upon old acquaintances from the States, and were introduced to many Honolulans. Some of these were Hawaiian or part-Hawaiian, who met us with a half-bashful, affectionate child-sweetness that was altogether irresistible. There is that in their beautiful eyes which calls for a like honesty and good-will and well-meaning.

Every one shakes hands—men, women, children —at every friendly excuse of meeting and parting. Smiles are one with the language, and there is a pretty custom of ending a remark, or even a direction, or command, with a pleasant " eh ! " —the *e* pronounced *a*, with an upward inflection. Jack is especially taken with this gentle snapper, and goes about practising on it with great glee.

You might have thought yourself at a social fair at home, what of the canopies, refreshments, and familiar faces of countrymen—but for ·the interspersing of brown Hawaiians, so soft and

so velvet in face and body, voice and movement,
" the friendliest and kindest people in the world."
A learned New Englander over forty years ago
wrote : " When the instinct of hospitality which
is native to these islands gets informed and en-
riched and graced by foreign wealth, intelligence,
and culture, it certainly furnishes the perfection
of social entertainment. Of course there are in
other lands special circles of choice spirits who
secure a brilliant intercourse all to themselves of
a rare and high kind, but I question if anywhere
in the whole world general society is more attractive than in Honolulu. Certainly nowhere else
do so many nationalities blend in harmonious
social intercourse. Natives of every well-known
country reside there, and trading vessels or war-
ships from America and the leading countries of
Europe are frequently in port. A remarkable
trait of these foreign-born or naturalized Hawaiians
is that interest in their native land seems only
intensified by their distant residence. The
better Hawaiians they are, the better Americans,
English, French, or Germans they are. And thus
it happens that you meet people fully alive to
the great questions and issues of the day all the
world over. Their distance from the scene of
these conflicts seems to clear their view, and I
have heard some of the wisest possible comments
upon American affairs, methods, and policies
from residents of the islands. Besides, they have
in small the same problems to solve in their little
kingdom which engage us. All the projected

reforms, social, moral, civil, or religious, have
their place and agitators here."

The residence of the Prince and Princess was
open to the public, and we roamed through a
labyrinth of handsome apartments, now up a step
into a big drawing-room furnished in magnificent
native woods and enormous pots of showering
ferns, the walls hung with old portraits in oil
of the rulers of Hawaii ; now down three steps
into a pillared recess where, in a huge iron safe,
unlocked for the evening, we were shown various
trophies of the monarchies.   Near by were several
tremendously valuable old royal capes woven of
tiny bird-feathers, some red, some of a rich deep
yellow, and others of the two colours combined in
a glowing orange.   In still another apartment, a
glass-front cabinet displayed shelf after shelf of
medals and trinkets pertaining to the past regime,
including the endless decorations received by
King David Kalakaua in the lands visited in
his progress around the world.   Some one had
remarked that he possessed more of these royal
decorations than any known monarch.   But this
is not so surprising as the fact that he was the
only known reigning monarch who ever circum-
navigated the globe.   This was in the early '80s.
His visit to Japan was not entirely for adventure,
but had a deeper intent, and the royal house of
Nippon will long remember the jolt it received
from the merry but purposeful King.   For
Kalakaua's brain was a busy one, and, having no
heart to see his realm absorbed by his white

neighbours on the Continent, he conceived an alliance with what seemed a less alien people, who had already in great numbers migrated to his shores. In company with him travelled his American Chamberlain, Colonel C. H. Judd, and his Attorney-General, William N. Armstrong. Successfully concealing from them his deep-laid plot, one day he walked out of the Tokio Palace allotted for his entertainment, and bearded the astounded but courteous Mikado in his royal house, with the carefully-considered project of an alliance between the Crown Prince of Japan and his own niece, and heir to the throne of Hawaii, the beautiful and accomplished Princess Victoria Kaiulani, daughter of his sister, Princess Miriam Likelike and the Honourable A. S. Cleghorn. But the Mikado, flower of an ancient and intricate civilization, did not see his way to a union of his blood with that of a people, no matter how promising nor how brilliantly represented by its own blue-blooded ruler, who were less than sixty years in the march of civilization ; and because he did not see the light that had illumined his dusky caller's very cosmopolitan thought-processes, the United States, instead of Japan, is now in possession of the finest naval station in the Pacific, if not in the world—Pearl Harbour.

A space in the fascinating cabinet was devoted to the Crown of the Realm, a piece of workmanship at once formal and barbaric, with its big bright gems, most conspicuous of which, to me, were the huge pearls. One diamond had been stolen, and the large gaping socket was a pathetic reminder of the empty throne in the old Palace which is now the Executive Building.

Many and barbaric were the objects in this modern home, mere " curios " should the uncaring gaze upon them in a museum ; but here in Hawaii they breathed of the pomp of a vanishing race whose very hands we were pressing and whose singers' living voices caressed the heavy, fragrant air ; the while across a lawn that had been carpet for Hawaii Nei festivities of many years, sat the rebellious deprived Queen under the eaves of a grass house.

When, we wonder, in our westward traverse, shall we see another queen, or a prince, or a princess—even shadows of such as are these of Hawaii ? Not soon enough, I swear, to fade the memory of this remarkable trio ; for nothing can ever dim the picture that is back of our eyes. And the Princess Elizabeth Kalanianaole has set an example, a pattern, that will make us full critical of royal women of any blood.

SEASIDE HOTEL, WAIKIKI BEACH,
HONOLULU, *May* 31, 1907.

" Waikiki ! there is something in the very name that smacks of the sea ! " carolled a visitor in the late '70s. Waikiki—the seaside resort of the world, for there is nothing comparable to it, not only in the temperature of its effervescent water, which averages 78° the year round, but

in the surroundings, as well as the unusual variety
of sports connected with it, surf-canoeing in the
impressively-savage black and yellow dug-outs,
surf-boarding, the ancient game of kings, fishing,
sailing ; and all on a variously shallow reef, where
one may swim and romp forgetful hours without
necessarily going out of depth on the sandy
bottom.   The cream-white curve of beach is for
miles feathered with coco-nut palms, and Dia-
mind Head, " Leahi," that loveliest of old craters,
which rounds in the south-eastern end of the
graceful crescent, is painted by every shifting
colour, light, and shade, the day long, on its rose-
tawny, serrated steeps.   And many's the sail
comes whitening around the point, yacht or
schooner or full-rigged ship, a human mote that
catches the eye and sets one adreaming of lately
hailed home harbours and far foreign ports
with enchanting names.

Waikiki ! Waikiki ! We keep repeating the
word, for already it spells a new phase of existence.
Here but a scant twenty-four hours, and already
Jack's Dream Harbour seems faint and distant,
slipping into a mild and pleasant, not imperative
memory, for the spirit of storied Waikiki has
entered ours.   The air seems full of wings, I am
so happy making home, this time a tent !   We two
can pitch home anywhere we happen to light : a
handful of clothes-hangers, some paper and a
supply of Jack's chubby ink-pencils—and other
details are mere incidentals, for home is in our
hearts.   After all, perhaps the art of living, great-

est of arts, may be partially summed up in this wise :—

> . . . to inhabit the earth is to love that
> which is ; to catch the savour of things.

This domicile is a brown tent-house, comprising three rooms separated by thin *portières*, with an accessory bath-house and servant-room, also of tenting, and is the last of a scattered row of outside accommodations belonging to the Seaside Hotel, some of them weathered old cottages whose history one would love to know.   A short distance *mauka*, as every one says for " mountainward," or away from *makai* (toward the sea), on a lawn pillared with sky-brushing coco-nut palms, still stands a true old grass house of romantic history.   It was created for the seaside retreat of King Lot, Kamehameha V, during his reign in the decade commencing 1863, and each Wednesday was devoted to the fashioning of it, from *Lama* wood inside and pandanus leaves outside.   It was named Lama House, for the wood was ordinarily sacred to the temples and construction of idols in the older days.   Kamehameha V left no issue, and upon his death the estate went to the Princess Ruta (Ruth) Keelikolani, and at her demise to Mrs. Bernice Pauahi Bishop, the last descendant of Kamehameha the Great.

To the south we are separated from the big Moana Hotel with its tiers of green roofs, which is fairly empty and quiet between steamer arrivals, by a sand-banked stream fed from the mountains, with, beyond, a lavender field of lilies.   Kalakaua

Avenue is so far away across our hotel gardens that the only sound from that quarter is an occasional rumble of electric trams crossing a bridge over the stream, fitting into our bright solitude like distant thunder from the black range that we glimpse through a grove of palms and algaroba.

Not twenty feet in front, where grass grows to the water's edge at highest tide, the sands, sparkling under blazing sunrays, are frilled by the lazy edges of the surf ; and the flawed tourmaline of the reef waters, pale green, or dull pink from underlying coral patches, stretch to the low white line of breakers on the barrier reef some half-mile seaward, while farthest beyond lies the pea-cock-blue ribbon of the deep-sea horizon.

In the cool of morning we skipped across the prickly grasses for a dip, accompanied by a frisking collie neighbour. The water was even more wonderful than at the Lochs, invigorating enough at this early hour, full of life and movement. Jack gave me lessons in diving through the mild breakers, and it was hard to tear ourselves away, even for the tempting breakfast tray that a white-suited Filipino was bearing to the tent-house.

While I write, Jack, in his beloved old blue kimono, sits working in a draughty spot he has hunted in the front room. As for the kimono, it is limp and shabby from many launderings ; '' But I love the old thing,'' he says, '' although, if you'll buy me a new one next time you're in town, I promise to wear it.'' He is commencing

D

an article on amateur navigation, for *Harper's*, which he calls " Finding One's Way About." This is the second article of a series for *Harper's* on the *Snark* venture. The first, written at sea and entitled " The Inconceivable and Monstrous " deals with the building of his much-sinned-against craft. The name of the article should be an incitement to read. He declares that these articles will be the only ones concerning the actual voyage, handling the various striking phases of the experience ; otherwise he will devote his energies to fiction—his creative man-work, while I am to keep the diary.

One reason why Jack has concluded to limit his writing upon the voyage itself, is because the eastern magazine that first contracted to buy the same immediately started a pernicious advertising to the effect that it was sending the *Snark* around the world ! This naturally incensed Jack, who was paying dearly out of his own pocket with deadly-hard work, in the chaotic condition of things succeeding the earthquake, to prepare the vessel for the sea. The magazine tried to get back at him for his prompt stand against such advertising by attacking his good faith in arranging with a woman's magazine for a set of land-articles on domestic customs of women and children in the islands we should visit ; whereupon Jack, a bonnie fighter, perfectly clear in his own mind as to his intent and honesty, refused to do any voyage articles whatever. To fulfil the con-tract, in place of the mooted yachting articles, he offered a string of autobiographical studies of his tramping days across the United States ; and these were indignantly but avidly accepted by the editor, who was " in wrong " and knew it, and who had to make good to his magazine.   Jack is still giggling over the fury of the editor, who was so altogether out of sorts that in an inexplicable humour he offered a higher price for the substitute work—which, not surprisingly, was accepted before he had a chance to catch his breath.   The autobiographical sketches are now running under the title of " My Life in the Underworld," although Jack's caption was " The Road," which will be the name of the book when issued.

Mayhap I have been trying to do too much in this unaccustomed climate, for the long ride yesterday from Pearl Lochs left me very tired. The trade-wind has died again, and the only breeze was what our speed might afford.   Speeding for breeze on a Kona day is enervating for man and beast.   But we enjoyed the ride, for the two small mares, with regular use, have become very docile to wrist and heel.   Once in Honolulu there was difficulty in coaxing them past their home street ; but we soon had them trotting briskly along the three miles of King Street and Kalakaua Avenue to Waikiki.   This afternoon the Diamond Head road is to be our final ride.   Present plans are too uncertain to warrant our keeping the horses.

Mr. Fred Church, manager of the Seaside, is a really-truly acquaintance of Jack's Yukon days.

There are so many claimants who are not really-truly—although Jack has never " given away " a mother's son of them, on occasion when they have been dragged up by fond relatives to make good their assertions. " Let 'm have their fun,". he laughs, " it doesn't hurt me any. It's awful to be called down in front of one's women-folk ! " There are instances when I cannot quite approve of the length to which he carries this policy, for very nasty tales have based upon his easy in-dulgent, " Oh, sure, I remember ! " to some perfect stranger who has bragged, " Don't you remember that time you and I . . . ? " when I knew that Jack and I together were elsewhere at the dates mentioned. But little he cares for the opinions except of a close few—very few. Large-mindedly he lays himself open to all sorts of criticism and revilement—and gets it. " These aren't the things that count, Mate Woman," he reasons. " What you and I think and know are the big things. Besides," he usually sums up, " I have to sleep with myself, and I sleep well." So much for *his* good conscience.

But I was talking about this genuine Klondiker, Fred Church, our big, good-looking, breezy host, who, ably aided and abetted by his little beauty wife, makes the guest feel as if entertained in their private home—the very genius of hotel management. Mr. Church was full as cordial as the letters he had been sending from the day of our arrival, in which he had urged us to be his guests for all the privileges of the beach. Pleasure in the beach itself was doubled by the welcome of these two and their discerning choice of this sequestered little house of brown canvas and wire screening, swept by every wind that blows, from mauka or makai. Tired and warm as we were, their suggestion for a swim before dinner was just as exactly inspired as Gretchen Waterhouse's invitation to a hot tubbing.

Besides our cottage row, the Seaside Hotel comprises one large frame house of many rooms, half-over the water, reached by a winding driveway from the main avenue through a grove of lofty coco-nut palms, under which stray large cottages belonging to the hotel. In a rambling one-storied building are the kitchen, the bar, an Oriental private dining-room, and a reception hall also furnished in Chinese carved woods and splendid fittings, that belong to the estate. This hall opens into a circular lanai with frescoed ceiling—a round dining and ball-room open half its disk. Beyond the curving steps, on the lawn towards the sea, grow two huge gnarled *hau* trees, each in the centre of a round platform where drinks are served. The hau is a native of the islands, and is nearly related to the hibiscus. The limbs snarl into an impenetrable shade, and are hung with light yellow bells formed of eight to ten lobes, which turn to mauve and then to ruddy brown when they fall.

Dinner, served in the private room, was given by the Churches for us to meet some of Honolulu's young married pairs. They formed a glowing ring about the table, which Mrs. Church had decorated in poinsettia and red-shaded candles. Each woman present was distinctly handsome in her own way, and all were beautifully gowned and essentially " smart." Several of their husbands wore white and gold uniforms. But no one was more attractive than little Mrs. Church— pretty as a child or a doll, with the dignity of carriage that can make a small woman the stateliest in the world.

After the dinner, the dance—" Transport Night Dance." While the first word is appropriate for the bewitchment of dancing in a Hawaiian night to the music of Hawaii, it is here used to designate the entertainment on arrival of a United States Army Transport, when the officers and their ladies come ashore midway in the long passage to or from the coast and the Philippines.

The immense half-open circle of the lanai was cleared of dining equipment, and the shining floor dusted with shavings of wax. Many-hued Chinese lanterns were the only lighting in the lanai and out among the trees, where dancers rested in the pauses of the music.

And the music ! It was made entirely by a Hawaiian orchestra of guitars and ukuleles, with a piano for accent, and all I had heard and dreamed of the glamour of " steamer night in Honolulu " came to pass. It seemed hardly more real than the dream, gliding over the glassy floor to lilt of hulas played and sung by these brown musicians whose mellow, slurring voices sang to

the ukuleles and guitars because they could not
refrain from singing. Only one regret was in my
contentment—that Jack did not dance. Jack
never dances. " I never had time to learn," he
says, " and now I'm too old ! I'd rather keep cool
and watch you dance."

One of our party at dinner was Mrs. A. G.
Hawes, whose name, Francesca Colonna, is no
more gorgeously Italian than her great black
eyes and gold-banded black hair. Between two
dances she carried me off to a group at a table
under one of the hau trees, where I found Jack
already talking with Princess David Kawananakoa
and her husband, who is brother to Prince
" Cupid " and whom he resembles. This Princess,
Abigail, was a Campbell and is only about an
eighth Hawaiian. And oh, she is a beauty !—
no more splendid in port than her sister-in-law,
but much more European in colouring and feature.
Doubtlessly she could be quite as regal upon
occasion ; but this evenng she was charmingly
vivacious, and I caught myself looking with
affection born of the instant into her beautiful
eyes that smiled irresistibly with her beautiful
mouth—" a smile of pearls."

During a dance with an army officer, I quite
fittingly and very slightly cut my hand upon a
sword in a sheaf of swords decorating the central
column. My partner was greatly distressed and
apologetic, but I assured him that my first
military ball could not have been complete
without this sword-scratch.

An interesting incident of the evening was the meeting of Mrs. Francis Gay, of Kauai. Years ago, I used to see her and her sister, now Mrs. Jordan, travelling to and from Berkeley and San Francisco, music-rolls in hand, both daughters of Judge Hart, who had married a lady of Hawaii. Mrs. Gay is very handsome, with the eyes and mouth of her mother's people—sweet and caressing and gracious.

The lovely ball · closed with " Aloha Oe," " Love to You," in waltz measure, while the dancers joined in singing. The last, slow, dying cadence left one with a reposeful sense of fulfil-ment, and none broke this dreamy repose by clapping for an encore.

WAIKIKI,
Saturday, June 1, 1907.

Yesterday, after a luncheon that included our first *yam* (little different from and no better than a fried potato-patty), we rode to Diamond Head, where at last I gazed into my first crater. The way led through Kapiolani Park, where the little sleeping volcano formed a painted back-ground for the scattered trees and blossoming lily-ponds. Once out of the shady drive-ways, we sweltered on the rising white road in a windless glare.

It was a mud-volcano, this Leahi, and upon its oblong steep sides remain the gutterings of age-ago eruptions. While less than 800 feet high, at a distance it appears much higher. We had

had a never-to-be-forgotten view of it on our first
ride up to Honolulu, when, through a gap, we
looked across the tree-embowered city, and the
low red crater of Punchbowl—Puowaina ; and
far Diamond Head rose too ethereal in the shimmering atmosphere to be of solid earth thrown
up by ancient convulsions.

Skirting the south side of the Head, we tethered
our dripping horses, and on foot climbed the
light-coloured, limy wall, seething hot under the
midday sun. I arrived at the edge of the crater
sans heart and lungs, muscles quivering and eyes
dim. But what I there saw brought me back in
short order to my normal state of joy at being
alive. Compared with other wonders of Hawaii
Nei, probably this small hollow mountain should
be sung without trumpets. But I have not seen
Haleakala and Kilauea, Mauna Kea or Hualalai,
and lacked no thrills over my first volcano, albeit
a dead one. The bowl is a wonderfully symmetri-
cal oval, and may be half a mile long—we could
not judge, for the eye measures all awry these
incurving walls of tender green, cradling, far
beneath, the still green oval mirror of a lake-
let.

We rested our burned eyes well on the soft
green shell of earth before taking the scorching
way down to the horses, and decided that small-
boat travel is ill training for mountain-scaling
anywhere near the Southern Cross. Around
Diamond Head we continued, looking off across
blue bays and white beaches to Koko Head, very

innocent seen from the land by light of day, but full of omen by night when winds blow not and small *Snarks* drift too near wicked reefs. To-day the road led close by the Diamond Head Lighthouse and the signal station that telephoned our approach to Honolulu ; and we learned that it was wirelessed from the city to the island of Maui, where the Congressional Party hung 10,000 feet, on the lip of Haleakala's twenty-three-mile crater. How different from times when the only way of messages was by the watery miles separating the islands, in small sloops and schooners or outrigger canoes, and telephones had never been dreamed of.

On the way to return Mr. Rowell's mares, Jack took me aside to the transport wharf that I might see the departure of a vessel from Honolulu, for never, since his own experiences, has he spoken without emotion of this beautiful ceremonial. There is nothing like it anywhere else in the world.

The steamer decks were bowers of fragrant colour, as was the wharf, for the shoulders of the departing Congressmen and their womenfolk were high-piled with wreaths of ilima, of roses, of heliotrope, carnations, lilies, and scented green things, while the dense throng ashore was hardly less garlanded, and streams of flowers flowed back and forth on the gangways. A great humming of voices blent with the quivering strains of an Hawaiian orchestra on the upper deck, and now and again all lesser tuneful din drowned in a

patriotic burst from Berger's Royal Hawaiian
Band ashore. A wonderful and impressive scene
it was, not alone for beauty, but in a human way,
for the myriad faces of the concourse shaded from
white through all the browns to yellow skins,
mingling in good fellowship and oneness of spirit
in this hour of farewell to the lawmakers of
their common cause. And none of these wishing
Godspeed were more imposing nor charming
than the Hawaiians, from the two Princes and
their splendid consorts to the humblest of their
people. *Humblest* is wrong—there is no humility
in the breed. Their eyes look only an innocent
equality of sweet frankness, and their feet step
without fear the soil they can but still feel is their
dearest own.

Prince Cupid, the Delegate, received round
after round of cheers from the passengers as the
deep-mouthed siren called the parting moment,
and at the last, the native orchestra, descending
the gangway, joined with the wind instruments
in Queen Liliuokalani's own song, composed
during her eight months' imprisonment, sweetest
farewells and hopes for a returning " Aloha Oe."
The human being did not live whose heart was
not conscious of a nameless longing for he knew
not what. One ached with burden of all the
good-byes that ever were and ever will be, of all
the sailings of all the ships of all the world. I
looked up into Jack's face, and his eyes were
shining moist as he pressed my hand, knowing I
was as moved as he would wish.

O warp her out with garlands from the quays,

went through my mind when the vessel glided
slowly past the wharf, and the ropes of living
blossoms and network of wild-coloured serpentine
broke and fell into the water. Flowers filled the
air as they were tossed to and from the gay tiers
of the ship, many falling into the stream, until
she moved upon a gorgeous tapestry.

As the huge black transport cleared, suddenly
her surface seemed flying to pieces. A perfect
fusillade of small dark objects in human form
sprang from her sides, rails, rigging, from every
height of ringbolt and sill, and disappeared in
almost unrippling dives through the swirling
blossomy carpet of the harbour.

" Look—look-at-them ! " Jack cried, incoherent
with the excitement of his joy in the little kanaka
imps who entered the water so perfectly and came
up shaking petals from their curly heads, white
teeth flashing, and their child-faces eloquent with
expectation of a lucrative shower from the
passengers. A bountiful day it was for them,
and little their bright eyes and brown hands lost
of the copper and silver disks that slowly fell
through the bubbling flood. We both wished
we were down there with them, for it is great fun
to pick a coin from the deep as it filters down
with a short, angled, tipping motion.

" Do you wish you were aboard, going back ? "
Jack asked, as we turned for the last time to
look at the diminishing bulk of the transport,
bannered with scarves and handkerchiefs and

serpentine. I did not. I want to go home only from east to west. Who knows ? It may be through the Panama Canal !

In our tent-household, Jack is the only one who works. My typewriter was left behind at Pearl Lochs, and I do not allow myself to think of the hot, if interesting hours of copying upon returning. Such content is ours here at Waikiki that Jack says it is a shame to press it all into one life, for it could be spread over several incarnations. We sleep like babies, in the salt night-airs wafting through the mosquito canopies. Before break-fast, it is into the blissful warm tide, diving through bubbling breakers, and coming up eyes level with tiny sails of fishermen beyond the barrier reef. The pretty, pretty strand ! All hours one hears the steady gentle boom and splash of the surf— not the big disturbing, ominous gnashing and roaring of the Pacific Coast rollers, nor the dis-tant carnivorous growlings off the rock-jagged line of New England. And under sun or moon, it is all a piece of beauty. Toward Diamond Head, when the south wind drives, the swift breakers, like endless charges of white horses, leap and surge shoreward, flinging back long silver manes. The thrill of these landward races never palls at Waikiki. One seems to vision Pharaoh's Horses in mighty struggle against backwashing waters, arriving nowhere, dying and melting impotent upon the sand.

Jack, to whom beauty is never marred by knowledge of its why and wherefore, has explained to me the physics of a breaking wave.

"A wave is a communicated agitation," says he. "The water that composes a wave really does not move. If it moved, when you drop a stone in a pool and the ripples widen in an increasing circle, there should be at the centre an increasing hole. So the water in the body of a wave is stationary. If you observe a portion of the ocean's surface you will see that the same water rises and falls endlessly to the agitation communicated by endless successive waves. Then picture this communicated agitation moving toward shore. As the land shoals, the bottom of the wave hits first and is stopped. Water is fluid, and the upper part of the wave not having been stopped, it keeps on communicating its agitation, and moves on shoreward. Ergo," says he, "something is bound to be doing, when the top of a wave keeps on after the bottom has stopped, dropped out from under. Of course, the wave-top starts to fall, forward, down, cresting, over-curling and crashing. So, don't you see? don't you see?" he warms to his illustration, "it is actually the bottom of the wave striking against the rising land that causes the surf! And where the land shoals gradually, as inside this barrier reef at Waikiki, the rising of the undulating water is as gradual, and a ride of a quarter of a mile or more can be made shoreward on the cascading face of a wave."

Alexander Hume Ford, true to promise, ap-

peared to-day with an enormous surf-board, made
fun of the small ones that had been lent us, and
we went down to the sea to learn somthing of
hee-nalu, sport of Hawaiian kings.   The only
endeavour of fish, flesh, and fowl, which Mr. Ford
seems not to have partially compassed, is that
of the feathered tribe—undoubtedly from lack of
time, for his energy and ambition are tireless
enough even to grow feathers.   Jack, who himself seldom stops short of what he wants to accomplish, finds this man most stimulating in an un-
selfish enthusiasm to revive neglected customs of
elder islands days, for the benefit of Hawaii and
her advertisement to the outside world.   Although
we have seen a number of natives riding the
breakers, face downward, and even standing
upright, almost no white men seem to be expert.
Mr. Ford, born genius of pioneering and promot-
ing, swears he is going to make this island's pas-
time one of the most popular in the world, and,
judging by his personal valour, he cannot fail.

The thick board, somewhat coffin-shaped, with
rounded ends, should be over six feet long for
adults.   This plank is floated out to the breaking
water, which can be done either wading alongside
or lying face-downward paddling, and there you
wait for the right wave.   When you see it coming,
stand ready to launch the board on the gathering
slope, spring upon it, and—keep on going if you
can.   Lie flat on your chest, hands grasping the
sides of the large end of the heavy timber, and
steer with your feet.   The expert, having gauged

the right speed, rises cautiously to his knees, to full stature, and then, erect with feet in the churning foam, makes straight for the beach, rides up the sparkling incline, and steps easily from his arrested sea-car.

A brisk breeze this afternoon, with a rising surf, brought out the best men, and we saw some splendid natives at close range, who took our breath away with their reckless, beautiful performance. One, George Freeth, who is only one-quarter Hawaiian, is accounted the best surf-board rider and swimmer in Honolulu.

When a gloriously-bodied kanaka, naked but for a loin-cloth carved against his shining bronze, takes form like a miracle in the down-rushing smother of a breaking wave, arms outstretched and feet winged with feathers of backward-streaming spray, you watch, stricken of speech. And it is not the sheer physical splendour of the thing that so moves one, for lighting and informing this is an all-dominating spirit of joyful fearlessness and freedom that manifests an almost visible soul, and that lends a slow thrilling of awe to one's contemplation of the beauty and wonder of the human. What was it an old Attic philosopher exclaimed? "Things marvellous there are many, but among them all naught moves more truly marvellous than man."

And our journalist friend, malihini, white skinned, slim, duplicated the act, and Jack murmured, "Gee! What a sport he is—and what a sport it is for white men too!" His glowing eyes, and a well-known firm expression about the jaw, told me he would be satisfied with nothing less than hours a day in the deep-water smokers. As it was, in the small surf, he came safely in several times. I accomplished one successful landing, slipping up the beach precisely to the feet of some stranger hotel guests, who were not half [so surprised and embarrassed as myself. I took some while to learn to mount the board without help, for it is a cumbrous and unruly affair in the lively water.

The rising tide was populous with Saturday afternoon bathers, but comparatively few women, exceptclose inshore. A fleet of young kanaka surf-boarders hovered around Ford and his haole pupils, for he loves children and is a great favourite with these. Often, timing our propelling wave, we would find a brown and smiling cherub of ten or so, all eyes and teeth, helpfully timing the same wave, watching with altruistic anxiety lest we fail and tangle up with the pitching slice of hardwood. Not a word would he utter—but in every gesture was " See ! See ! This way ! It is easy ! "

Several times, on my own vociferous way, I was spilled diagonally adown the face of a combing wave, the board whirling as it overturned and slithering up-ended, while I swam to bottom for my very life, in fear of a smash on the cranium. And once I got it, coming up wildly, stars shooting through my brain. And once Jack's board, on which he had lain too far forward, dived, struck bottom, and flung him head over heels in the most ludicrous somersault. His own head was struck in the ensuing mix-up, and we were able to compare size and number of stars. Of course, his stars were the bigger—because my power of speech was not equal to his. It seems to us both that never were we so *wet* in all our lives, as during those laughing, strenuous, half-drowned hours.

Sometimes, just sometimes, when I want to play the game beyond my known vitality, I almost wish I were a boy. I do my best, as to-day; but when it comes to piloting an enormous weighty plank out where the high surf smokes, above a depth of twelve to fifteen feet, I fear that no vigour of spirit can lend my scant five-feet-two, short hundred-and-eleven, the needful endurance. Mr. Ford pooh-poohs : " Yes, you can. It's easier than you think—but better let your husband try it out first."

Late in the day there came to the tent-house a solid, stolid sailorman of fifty or so, giving his name as Captain Rosehill, and asking for a berth in the *Snark*. Jack talked with him at some length, and finally advised him to look over the *Snark* carefully before making up his mind, giving him to understand that there is more than mere navigating to do aboard so small a vessel, and that before we are able to sail from Hawaii he will be sure to find plenty of work in the matter of making her ready. Rosehill evidently knows Schwank, for when that worthy's name was mentioned, he gave a prodigious sniff which died in a grunt. The only time the man smiled was at leaving. Upon inquiry, we find that his melancholy is not without justification, for beyond discussion he is " king " of Marcus Island, a small guano principality that he discovered in 1889 somewhere between Bonin Islands and the Carolines. Jack was interested in the facts for themselves, and also because he landed in that section of the world during his voyage in the *Sophie Sutherland*, which made a call at Bonin Islands. Through a mix-up with the Japanese Government, Rosehill was defrauded of indefinite millions that he might have harvested from the guano deposit. They say he knows the South Seas like a book, and is a good navigator. Nothing would make Jack happier than to be free to devote himself to the navigation of his own boat, for if there is one place above all others where he is more contentedly at home, it is at sea. But a sailing-master he must have, and the right man will lift a small world of responsibility from his shoulders.

WAIKIKI,
Sunday, June 2, 1907.

An eventful day, this, especially for Jack, who is in bed thinking it over between groans, eyes puffed, shut with a strange malady, and agonizing in a severe case of sunburn. I can sympathize to some extent, for, in addition to a considerable roasting, my whole body is racked with muscular quirkings and lameness from the natatorial gymnastics of the past forty-eight hours. Our programme to· day began at ten, with a delirious hour of canoe-riding in a pounding surf. While less bold individual valour is called upon, this game is even more exciting than surf-boarding, for more can take part in the shoreward rush.

The great canoes are themselves the very embodiment of royal barbaric sea-spirit—dug whole out of hard koa logs, long, narrow, over two feet deep, with very slightly curved perpendicular sides and rounded bottoms ; furnished with steadying outriggers on the left, known as the " i-à-ku "—two long curved timbers, of the light tough hardwood, with their outer ends fastened to the heavy horizontal spar, or float, of wili-wili, called the " a-ma." The hulls are painted · dull, dead black, and trimmed by a slightly in-set, royal-yellow inch-rail, broadening upward at each end of the boat, with a sharp tip. There is an elegance of savage war-likeness about these long black shapes ; but the sole warfare in this day and age is with Neptune, when, manned by shining bronze crews, they breast or fight through the oncoming legions of rearing, trampling, neighing sea-cavalry.

It required several men on a side to launch our forty-foot canoe across sand into the shoring tide, and altogether eight embarked, vaulting aboard as she took the water, each into a seat only just wide enough. Jack wielded a paddle, but I was put into the very bow, where, both out and back, the sharpest thrills are to be had. As the canoe

worked seaward in the high breaking flood, more
than once breath was knocked out of me when the
bow lunged right into a stiff wall of green water
just beginning to crest. Again, the canoe poised
horizontally, at right angles to the springing
knife-edge of a tall wave on the imminence of
over-curling, and then, forward-half in mid-air,
plunged head-into the oily abyss, with a prodigious
slap that bounced us into space, deafened with
the grind of the shore-going leviathan at our backs.
I could hear Jack laughing in the abating tumult
of sound, as he watched me trimming my lines
so as to present the least possible surface to the
next briny onslaught. He knew, despite my
desperate clutches at the canary streak on either
hand, and my uncontrolled noise, that I was having
the time of my life, as, from his own past experience, he had told me I would have.

It was more than usually rough, so that our
brown crew would not venture out as far as we
had hoped, shaking their curly heads like serious
children at the big white water on the barrier
reef. Then they selected a likely wave for the
slide beachward, shouting strange cries to one
another that brought about the turning of the
stern seaward to a low green mounting hill
that looked half a mile long and ridged higher
and higher to the burst.

" A hill, a gentle hill, Green and of mild declivity
. . . It is not ! " Fred Church quoted and com-
mented on his Byron and the threatening young
mountain, with firm hands grasping his paddle,

when, at exactly the right instant, he joined the frantic shrill " *Hoē!   Hoē!* " (*Paddle! paddle like—everything!*) that sent all paddles madly flying to maintain an equal speed with the abrupt, emerald slope.   Almost on end, *wiki-wiki, faster-faster, and yet faster*, we shot, ever the curl of white water behind, above, overhanging, menacing any laggard crew.   Once I dared to look back. Head above head I glimpsed them all; but never can fade the picture of the last of all, a magnificent Hawaiian sitting stark in the stern, hardly breathing, curls straight back in the wind, his biceps bulging to the weight of canoe and water against the steering-paddle, his wide brown eyes reflecting all the responsibility of bringing right-side-up to shore his haole charge.

And then the stern settles a little at a time, as the formidable seething bulk of water dissipates upon the gentle up-slope of the land before the Moana, while dripping crew and passengers swing around in the backwash and work out to repeat the manœuvre.

Few other canoes were tempted into the surf to-day, but we saw one capsize by going crookedly down a wave.   The yellow outrigger rose in the air, then disappeared in crashing white chaos. Everything emerged on the sleek back of the comber, but the men were unable in the ensuing rough water to right the swamped boat.   We lost sight of them as the next breaker set us inshore, but on subsequent trips saw them swimming slowly in, towing the canoe bottom upward, like a black dead sea-monster, and apparently making a picnic of their disaster.

An hour of this tense and tingling recreation left us surprisingly tired, as well as cold from the strong breeze on our wet suits and skins. Mr. Ford, with a paternal " I-told-you-so " smile at our enthusiasm over the canoeing, was prompt for the next event on our programme, which was a further lesson in surf-boarding. After helping me for a time, I noticed he and Jack were sending desireful glances toward the leaping backs of Pharaoh's Horses, and I knew they wanted to be quit of the pony breakers inshore—the wahine surf, as the native swimmers have it, and manful-wise ride the big water. Our friend had a thorough pupil in Jack, who with characteristic abandon never touched foot to bottom in four broiling midday hours.

Nursing my own reddened skin in the cool tent-house, I saw a weary figure dragging its feet across the lawns, which it was hard to recognize for Jack until he came quite near. Face and body, he was covered with large swollen blotches, like hives, and his mouth and throat were closing painfully. Rather against his wish, I sent Tochigi to summon a doctor, for his condition was alarming. Despite full knowledge of his extremely sensitive skin, he had not given a thought during those four hours, face downward on the board, to the fact that under the vertical rays of a tropic sun a part of him never before so exposed was being cooked through and through. Shoulders and back of neck were cruelly grilled, goodness knows ; but the really frightful damage had been wreaked on the backs of his legs, especially the tender hind-side of the knee joints, which were actually warping from the deep burning so rapidly that in a few moments he could not stand erect because the limbs refused to straighten. Between us, we managed to get him into bed, and later on, restless with the intolerable pain of his ruined surfaces, and thinking my room might be cooler, he could progress there only on *heels and palms, face upward*. " Don't let me laugh—it hurts too much," he moaned through swollen lips, realizing the preposterous spectacle.

Little aid could be rendered either of diagnosis or practice by the physician, Dr. Charles B. Cooper. From his six-feet-odd of height he bent wide black eyes upon the piteous mass on my bed, that indisputably required all known sun-burn remedies ; but the extraordinary swollen blotches were plainly beyond him. He had observed cases of mouth and throat swelling, though never one so bad as this, from fruit-poisoning in the tropics ; but this patient had eaten nothing that he had not been living on for weeks. And also there was the blotched body.

" Just my luck ! " this from the sufferer. " I'm always running into something no one ever saw or heard of ! Although this is something like the shingles I had on the *Sophie Sutherland*."

Dr. Cooper left some medicine, and later his

filled prescription came from a druggist, to relieve the torturing burn. Meantime I kept up a steady changing of cool wet cloths on the warped legs, while Jack's " It can't last for ever ! " was the best cheer under the circumstances, until the blotches began to subside and the throat could swallow grateful draughts of cold water and a supper of long, iced poi-cocktail—" Such beneficent stuff," he dwelt upon it.

You ! All whiteskins who would learn Ford's rejuvenescent royal sport, take warning that the " particular star " which illumines our world, despite its insidiousness, is particularly ardent in Hawaiian skies.

PEARL LOCHS,
Tuesday, June 6, 1907.

Home in our Dream Harbour, after a full week away—for of course Jack could not return on Monday as planned. The burning hours were beguiled with cool cloths and reading aloud, Jack taking his turn when I grew nervous with my own distressed cuticle and an aching ear from diving. Out of his grip of varied reading matter, he had selected Lilian Bell's *The Under Side of Things*—I wonder if with reference to his fried-and-turned-over condition ! A *Bulletin* reporter lightened a half-hour in an interview upon our unplotted future around the globe, and told us that our erstwhile sailing master, leaving yesterday for the coast on the Sierra, had given the impression that he considered the *Snark* unsafe.

" He built her ! " was Jack's only comment.

" And sailed over 2000 miles in her," the newspaper man grinned.

On Tuesday, waiving all discussion, Jack got into his clothing, the operation (not an inappropriate word) accompanied by running commentary on things as they were, which would be both interesting and instructive in a biographical sense, did one dare the editorial censor. Neither of us was this day " admirin' how the world was made," and my full sympathy was with his fevered sentiments concerning astronomy, geology, the starry hereafter, mid-Pacific watering places—and Alexander-Hume-Fords.

" But I warned you, and warned you ! " fended poor Ford, suppressing an involuntary snicker as the fervid cripple, now on his feet, essayed a step or two. " And you're luckier than I was the first time I got burned—worse than you are—and by mistake used capsicum vaseline on my skin ! And anyway, I really did think you had become toughened a bit on your month at sea."

With stiff-crooked legs, for he could neither unbend nor further bend the knees, and feet pitched some twenty inches apart, Jack's action was perforce unlike that of any known biped. So enamoured did he become of the wonder of it that he insisted upon employing it to progress to the lanai for luncheon, where his most pitying acquaintances failed to keep back their laughter.

Be assured he enjoyed it all as much as they, for the lessening hurt made him very happy. An hour face-downward on the beach that fateful afternoon had not improved my own carriage, but I was not unwilling to risk it on a short trip along Kalakaua Avenue to the Aquarium, which Jack, from his memories, had pronounced a world-wonder. With many jibes at his remarkable gait, the Churches helped him aboard a car, and in the cool, many-roomed grotto, built of quarried coral, we forgot all earthly dole, spell-bound before the incredible forms and colours of the sentient rainbows.

It is impossible to communicate any adequate idea of these colour-organisms. If anything could be laughably lovely, any one of these would serve ; Striped Roman scarf effects showed behind the glass as if in a shop window display ; polka-dot patterns in colour schemes beyond imagining ; against the glass lay figured designs that manufacturers would make no mistake in copying ; and all were possessed of an iridescent quality that made one expect them to melt into the shifting greens of their element, as they dimmed in the farther spaces of the tanks. But presently they would intensify, coming on larger and brighter like marine head-lights in Elfland.

One fish was an aquatic bird-of-paradise for hues, with a long spine like an aigrette springing from midway of a body almost as round as a coin and not much larger, with golden-brown beak and large black eye. His name was the kihi-kih.

The hamaleanokuiwi was a turquoise-blue, five-inch shuttle, terminating in a peacock-blue wisp of tail, with fins like ruffles tipped with stripes of yellow and black, and a long blue needle for mouth. The little fins back and below its beaded eyes were tiny azure butterflies striped two-ways with purple and gold; and on each side the turquoise body a splotch of opaque gold lay like a sunbeam. Around this bright blue marvel slowly wove one of a magenta as vivid, and half as long, of familiar shape but with the eye of a frog shaded by a thick ruby lid, two pale pink fins shaped like centre-boards, and a dorsal fin with five smartly raked masts.

The kikakapu did not look his bristly name at all, but was a shapeless handful of pigments—pale green as a parrot, with bird-like head of harlequin opal and parrot-eye of black and yellow. Half of his dorsal was a black-velvet spot rimmed with gold, his tail two shades of grey with a root of scarlet. I haven't patience to spell the name of an almost perfect oval of blue black, with a flaming autumn-leaf on each side, a narrow dorsal of shaded rose and salmon-yellow bearing a dotted line of red, and a grey and red flag for tail, while two sapphire-blue feathers trailed underneath. Next him flaunted a canary-yellow fish that had patently been scissored mid-length and grown a stiff mauve tail in the middle of its vertical rear, to match a mauve-velvet, long-beaked face. A canary-wing formed this one's dorsal fin, and two absurd

back-slanted spikes and a ribby trailer decorated
its horizontal base.

The opule and the luahine were both meant
to be normally-formed—the first, speckled on
top like a mountain trout, its frills red and black
and blue, jaw crimson-spotted, with grass-green
gills and tiny gilt fins, and on its dark sides three
parallel rows of larger dots, and one dropped
below, of startling blue, each with an electric
light behind ! The second, all brown save for a
scarlet headlight on the tall dorsal, was simil-
arly lit up all over, fins as well, the head zig-
zagged with lightning-streaks of the same electric-
blue. The akilolo wore these cold blue jewels
set on plum satin, with electric-green stripes on
its head, crimson and green fins and sharply
demarked rudder of bright yellow.

One was a lovely thing, and would have been
a little heart of gold, if its white-and-gilt tail
had not transformed it into a perfect ace of
spades. Another, modestly shaped, bore pink
fins socketed in emerald like the head and tail,
a yellow stomach, seal-brown back, with three
broad downward bands of the emerald joining
a wide lateral band of the same, decorated in
hollow squares of indigo ! I'm telling you, as
Jack would say. There were also dainty mother-
of-pearl forms, and gorgeous autumnal petals of
the ocean drifting among the jewelled swimming
things, with little rainbow crabs lying on the
bottom of sand and shells, among other crannied
creatures.

An imaginative child could spin unending day-dreams about these living pictures in the cool grottoes of the Honolulu Aquarium ; and for nightmares, there are excellent specimens of the octopus family.   These squid we have on the Pacific Coast, but there is no way of observing them.   Mr. Potter, the superintendent, said his were unusually active to-day, and we saw them displaying all their paces—a very useful spectacle for those who may venture among the more unfrequented coral hummocks at Waikiki. A wader can be made very uncomfortable by their ugly ability to attach to a rock and a victim at one and the same time.   They showed their fighting colours through the glass, coming straight at us, their little devil's heads set with narrow serpent-eyes glinting maliciously, and sharp turtle-beaks, all their tentacles—awful constricting arms covered with awful suckers— cast behind in the lightning dart.

When attacked, the squid opens an " ink-bag," fouling the water to the confusion of its enemy.   A native in trouble with one, tears right into this ink-bag with his own teeth, and to this mortal wound the pediculate marine dragon gives up the ghost.   The only thing about the squid that is not unpleasant, to say the mildest, is its colour—in action a rosy-tan ; but when curled in the rock crevices, protective colouring makes it hard to detect.   Mr. Potter dropped some tiny crabs into the tank from behind the scenes, which caused an exhibition not soon to be forgotten. The almost invisible squid, watching with one bright eye, unwreathed its eight flexile, trailing limbs, rose swiftly, swooped, and enfolded the prey as with a swirl of net or veiling. When the monster presently unwound, the mites of crabs had been entirely absorbed.

" And the Creator sat up nights inventing that," Jack observed, with sacrilegious gravity. slowly shaking his head. The superintendent looked appropriately startled, but not unappreciative.

This Honolulu Aquarium, though small, is said to surpass in the beauty of its exhibit anything in the world, not excepting the Italian ; and fancy our surprise to learn that it is not maintained by the territory, nor yet by the city, existing solely by the enterprise of the electric railway company. The " coloured " fish are recruited from the chance catch in nets of native fishermen. It is not easy to understand why Honolulu is lukewarm with regard to this, one of her greatest attractions. Mr. Ford should be spoken to about it !

And Hawaii is a paradise for the visiting fisherman, where can be hooked anything from a shark to small-fry of various sorts, whether " painted " or otherwise. Among the many game salt-water fish may be named black sea-bass, barracuda in schools, albacore, dolphin, swordfish, yellowtail, amber fish, leaping tuna and several other kinds of tuna—all these fish of unthinkable weight and size. And flying fish may be picked off with rifle or shot-gun—or netted as with the old Hawaiians.

Ever keen on the trail of Why and Wherefore, Jack has left no stone of research unturned as to the cause of the violent swelling that succeeded his sunburning, and has finally diagnosed it as urticaria.

Glad are we to rest once more in our Sweet Home, in sight of that bright reminder of the long voyage yet to be, the *Snark* and her unwonted clatter of active repairs. For Captain Rosehill has accepted the commission, and " dry bones are rattling," as Jack chuckled a moment ago from the hammock. The sad old sea-dog has taken hold with a vengeance, but professes little respect for all the modern " fol-de-rol of gewgaws " that he found lying around, costly labour-saving gear, unavailing only because of the ruinous mis-handling it received in the post-earthquake days of building. He scoffs any notion that the vessel will refuse to heave-to under proper conditions, contending that we could not have had enough wind that night she failed. Standing with huge-limp-hanging arms, he almost half-smiled at our sea-anchor—an article he has always yearned to possess. Clearly it is the one thing aboard with which he is satisfied.

Jack finds endless source of amusement in his skipper and the irrepressible Schwank, who, he has learned, once sailed together. The experience evidently has not endeared one to the other, and

all our gravity is taxed when the pair display
their divergent ways of showing mutual dislike and contempt. Rosehill is a man of few
words; but words are not needed when Schwank's
name is mentioned. The sound of that raucous
proper noun curdles the old sailor's sober and
asymmetrical features. On the other hand,
Schwank is voluble and expressive. .Never in
his wildest tales of that ill-starred voyage with
Rosehill has he hinted that he was ship's cook
under Rosehill. When he recounts how the
vessel was wrecked, one would conclude that
Schwank had been in command instead of the
other, and, in giving this intentional twist to
verity, he loses sight of the fact that it looks
much as if he, Schwank, must be responsible for
the loss. " I told Rosehill to brace up," he will
roar pompously, throwing a mighty chest. He
always appears about to rise triumphant from
the solid earth. Nor has he lost all of his piratical
tendencies. From his acre o fruitful soil, he
sells produce at extortionate prices. And he is
clever enough to vend these commodities through
his most beautiful offspring. When Maria-of-
the-Seraph-Smile, or Ysabel-of-the-Divine-Gaze
stands before me in the very artistry of colourful
tatters, proffering a scraggly pineapple or an
abortive tomato, valued at Israelitic sums, they
are not to be gainsaid. The pleasure is mine to
be robbed.

Martin finds quite a crowd to cook for, although
he reports that the captain eats little, and acts

E

as if he thinks less of the cook. We have an inkling
that the old man nurses a crusty disposition, for
the boys have already metamorphosed his pretty
name into " Raisehell "—not within his hearing,
I'll warrant. Soon or late there is going to be a
clash with Schwank—that is plain. " They're
too good to be true—they're classic sailormen.
May the best man win ! Rosehill has the hiring
and firing to do now," and Jack complacently
lights a cigarette—he has again taught himself
to smoke—and listens to the welcome music of
orders and the prompt obeying of same that come
on the shoreward breeze.

PEARL LOCHS,
Friday, June 7, 1907.

When you come to Hawaii, do not fail to visit
one of the big sugar plantations, to see the working
of this foremost industry of the territory, for
nowhere in the world has it been brought to
such perfection. Mr. Ford had arranged a trip
to the Ewa Plantation, a short distance by rail
south-west of the Lochs. With him came an
interesting young South African millionaire who
was much more bent upon discussing socialism
with Jack London than inspecting sugar mills—
although in the varied nationalities among the
labourers he might find a rare mine of sociologi-
cal data.

The railroad traverses a level stretch of country
dotted with pretty villages peopled by imported
human breeds. In my mind's eye lingers one

wee hamlet like a jewel in the sun—a group of little Portuguese shacks covered with brilliant flowering vines and hedged with scarlet hibiscus, all reflected to a verity in a still stream that brimmed even with its green banks. Not for nothing were these sunny-blooded children of Portugal blessed with wide and beautiful eyes ; for they can see no virtue in a dwelling that is not surrounded and entwined with living colour. No matter how squalid their circumstance, they do not rest until growing things begin to weave a covering of beauty.

Our station lay in the centre of the plantation, which embraces nearly 50,000 acres. It was the far-sighted father of Princess Kawananakoa, Mr. Campbell, who ten years ago bought this property for $1 an acre. Last year its output of sugar was over 29,000 tons. One alone of the underground pumping-plants which we wandered through, cost $180,000 ; and every day 70,000,000 gallons of water are pumped on this plantation.

Mr. Renton, the manager, devoted his day to our party. It must be more or less of a satis-faction, however, to a man of his patent capabili-ties, lord over the complicated affairs of such a project and its horde of workers, to display his achievement to men who can comprehend its enormousness and possibilities.

In comfortable chairs on a flat-car drawn by a small locomotive, over a network of tracks that intersect the property, we rode from point to point, meanwhile simmering gently in the moist hot air thick with an odour of growing cane, or, near the huge mill, of sugar in the making. The land reminded us of Southern California in spring-time, with tree-arboured roads and flower-drifted banks and fine irrigating ditches. We want to spend a day on horseback at Ewa, in the lanes and by-ways with their lovely vistas. Judging from Mr. Renton's own leisurely enjoyment of the occasion and frequent halting of the car that we might gather wild flowers and wild red toma-toes the size of cranberries, one would not have dreamed how busy a man he is.

It is hard, in the peaceful midst of this agri-cultural prospect, to realize that not long ago it was a dark place of pain and blood and terror. For here, 111 years ago, Kamehameha the Great dedicated a temple, *heiau*, with human sacrifices, preparatory to sailing for Kauai on conquest bent.

Sugar-cane is classified as a " giant perennial grass," but, unlike most members of the grass family, has solid stems, and grows from eight to twenty feet high. The origin of cane in these islands is unknown, although it is thought to have been introduced from the South Sea Islands by early native navigators in their questing canoes. It was used as an article of diet when white men first set foot in Hawaii, but not made into sugar until about 1828 ; and less than a decade after-ward the first exportation of sugar was shipped. Primitive stone rollers pressed out the sweet juice, and the boiling was done in crude iron

vessels.   Present-day processes have been brought
to a high state of scientific excellence, and probably no plant in the world has been so exhaustively
exploited.   The red lava soil, decomposed through
the ages, has been found through experimentation
to be the most productive, and the irrigation
scheme of one of these large plantations, with its
artesian wells and mountain reservoirs whence
water is carried great distances, is a tremendous
feat of engineering.

A man once wrote that agriculture in the tropics
consisted of not hindering the growth of things.
But the raising and converting into sugar of
these vast areas of rustling sugar-in-the-stem is
not such smooth luck.   He who would manufacture sugar has many formidable if infinitesimal
foes to success, among which **Mr. Renton**
named the nimble leaf-hopper, the cane-borer,
the leaf-roller, the mole-cricket, the mealy-bug,
the cypress girdler, and the Olinda-bug.   To discover the natural enemies of these pests requires
an able corps of entomologists seeking over the
face of the globe, as well as working sedulously
in the Experiment Station in Honolulu.

The mill itself, with its enormous processes,
I shall not attempt to describe further than to
assure you that it is a place of breathless interest
and wonder.   One sees the sugar, and tastes it,
in the succeeding phases of manufacture, up to
the point where it is shipped to the States for the
last stage of refining.

And more absorbing than these technicalities

of the plantation were the human races represented among the workers who live and labour, are born, are married, and die within its confines. Through a bewilder of foreign villages we wandered on foot—Japanese, Chinese, Portuguese, Norwegian, Spanish, Swedish, Korean; even the Russians were here but lately. Porto Ricans were tested, but proved a bad lot, always ready with a knife from behind. One cannot fail to note the scarcity of Hawaiian labourers—and rejoice in it, for they are proud and free creatures, and it would seem pity to bind them on their own soil. On the other hand, there is no gainsaying that they are capable toilers when they will. Indeed, it is said that they accomplish twice the work that a Japanese is willing to do in a day; but when pay day comes, the Hawaiian is likely not to appear again until all his money is gloriously spent. He is strong and trustworthy, and makes an excellent overseer, or *luna*, as well as teacher; for he is not merely imitative, but intelligent in applying what he has learned.

Mr. Renton led us into schools and kindergartens maintained for the scores of children, and presided over for the most part by white women. In one room we found a Japanese-Hawaiian teacher—a sweet and maidenly young thing, her Nipponese strain lending an elusive delicacy to the round, warm native features. In faultless English she explained the duties of her schoolroom, showing great pride in a sewing-class then in session, and pointing through the

window to where the boys of her class could be
seen putting the yard to rights.

I thought we could never leave the kindergartens, with their engaging babies of endless
colours and variety of lineaments, pure types and
cross-bred. Most beautiful of all were the
Portuguese, with only one drawback to their
childish' charm—the grave maturity of their
faces. Bella, however, two-years-tiny, golden-
eyed and gold-tawny of skin, forgot her temperamental soberness and coquetted shamelessly
from her absurd chair in the circle on the bright
floor, when she should have been attending to
teacher. But even Bella came to grief. Like
some other coquettes she was winningly familiar
at a distance ; and when I tried to cultivate a
closer acquaintance with the young pomegranate
blossom, and take a picture of her loveliness, she
fell victim to a panic of embarrassment and terror
that ended in violent weeping in teacher's lap.

Homeward bound, it seemed as if we had been
transported to and from a foreign land for the
day, although what land was the puzzle, in view
of the manifold types we had walked among.

Once more within our red wicket, we found
Gene just arrived from the coast steamer, and
were informed by the evening paper that he was
to accompany the *Snark* voyage for the purpose
of illustrating Jack London's books ! If only
he will illustrate that he can take care of the
engines, he will do more for us than could the
best black-and-white artist who ever drew.

In the soft black evening, some of the neighbours drifted across the yielding turf under the ancient trees, the women taking form softly in the velvet dark like tall spirit vestals trailing dim draperies and swirling incense. We lay out in the cool grass, the lighted ends of our scented punks flitting and darting like fireflies, and listened to Peer Gynt from the Victor indoors, and Mascagni's orchestral paradises of sound, Patti's rippling treble, and Emma Eames' clear fluting of " Still as the Night," floating upward to the sighing *obbligato* of a rising wind from across the rustling reef waters.

Sweet land of palms and peace, love and song— and yet, those who knew her in days gone by would walk sadly now in remembered haunts. Old faces are missing, and faces resembling them are few. The Hawaii of yesterday passes, and it makes even the stranger very pensive to see the changing. To one who views her from the height of his heart, a bright commercial future is cold compensation for the irreplaceable loss of the old Hawaii.

PEARL LOCHS,
Tuesday, June 11, 1907.

A bit of real Hawaii was ours last night— Hawaii as she is, with more than a trace of what she has been. It came about through an invitation from one of our neighbours, Mr. Moore, who owns the cemetery at Pearl City, to accompany his wife and himself to a native *luau* (loo-ah-oo—quickly, loo-ow), meaning feast. We four had the honour of being the only white guests, for in these latter days the natives are chary of including foreigners in their more intimate entertainments. But for Mr. Moore's confidential and sympathetic relation toward them, nothing would have induced them to consent to our intrusion.

The feast was a sort of " benefit," given at the christening of the baby of one of Mr. Moore's men, one " Willie," this being a familiar custom among the people. Mr. Willie and his pretty, giggly wife were in a small fine frenzy of hospitality and embarrassment at receiving a man who writes books, and ran out to the gate calling " Come in ! Come in ! Come in ! " in rapid sweet staccato.

We should have preferred to remain out-doors in their garden enclosure, which was decorated with palm fronds and flowers. But we were ushered to the cottage, where one glance into the hot little parlour, fainting with heavy-scented bouquets, every window sealed tight as if in a Maine winter, taught us that it was the pride of their simple, generous lives, with its neat furniture and immaculate " tidies " on chair and sofa and exact centre-table. Head and neck and shoulders, we were garlanded with ropes of buff-coloured ginger blossoms twined with mailé, and sat around straight-backed in delighted discomfort, wishing for fans. Admiring unstintedly the handsome slumbering infant who was the object and beneficiary of all the festival, we strove the while to express to our host and hostess how glad and proud we felt to be with them.

From the cool twilight lanai floated in to our ears the most bewitching, sleepy, sensuous music, rippled through with gurgles of lazy laughter. Presently, left to wander at will, whom should we discover in the happy huddle of musicians but Madame Alapai herself, not at all the grand prima of her Prince's gardens, but a warm, benevolent, smiling wahine, simply robed like all the rest in spotless white holoku, and unaffectedly ready, once her sudden, laughing bashfulness was conquered, to warble anything and everything she knew.

The coyness of these winsome brown women is only skin-deep, for to smiles and sincerity they warm and unfold like their own tropic blossoms to the morning sun. Deliciously they laugh at everything or nothing, with an abandon that does not tire, but draws the fascinated malihini fervently to wish he were one of them for the nonce—a product of sunshine and dew and love, without painful responsibility, with no care for the moment of aught but the living, loving present.

Madame Alapai accompanied the first American tour of the Royal Hawaiian Band, and the story runs that she was prepared to go on the second, but her husband, foolishly jealous of her successes and advantages, decided he needed a change of air and scene, and made the manager of his song-bird a proposition the prompt rejection of which

cost the band its *prima donna*. This proposition
was that he travel with the troupe and be paid a
salary for the honour of his mere company, since
he possessed no marketable talent. It seemed
sufficient to his limited vision that he should
allow his wife to earn *her* salary. Be it credited
the amiable lady that the facts were made public
without her assistance, for she remains guiltless
of shaming her life-companion by ridicule or
criticism. When asked why she did not go to the
coast the second time, she replies, with a slightly
lofty air that is without offence, what of its child-
likeness : " Oh, they wanted me to go, but I
refused."

She sang for us without reserve, out of her very
good repertory. Her voice is remarkable, and I
never heard another of its kind, for it is more
like a stringed instrument than anything I can
think of—metallic, but sweetly so, pure and
true as a lark's, with falls and slurs that are indes-
cribably musical and human. The love-eyed
men and women lounging about her with their
guitars and ukuleles, garlanded with drooping
roses and carnations and ginger, were commend-
ably vain of showing off their first singer in the
land, and thrummed their loveliest to her every
song. No one can touch strings as do these
people. Their fingers bestow caresses to which
wood and steel and cord become sentient and
tremblingly responsive.

The ukulele is the sweetest thing in the world—
that petite guitar-shape, with its four slender

strings, that seems a part of the native at every merry-making. It hailed originally from Portugal, but one seldom remembers this, so native has it become to the islands. The primitive Hawaiians played on a crude little affair that was a mere stick from the wood of the *ulei*, a sturdy flowering indigenous shrub. The tuneful stick was cut eighteen or twenty inches long and three or four wide, strung across with goat-gut, and was held in the teeth like a Jews'-harp, while the strings were swept with a fine grass straw. Lovers thus whispered through their teeth an understood language of longing and trysting, the light wood vibrating the voice to some distance in the still night.

From temporary arbours broke the clatter of busy wahines making ready the feast, and new guests laughed their way into the garden. Our nostrils twitched to unknown but appetizing odours. We expected as a matter of course that we should sit cross-legged on grass-mats while eating, and were disappointed to find a table prepared for the more distinguished of the company. At least I was disappointed; and Jack did not dare say he was glad of the white man's chair, but chuckled when I caught his eye from where he sat across the narrow board with Madame Alapai. Jack's friends know well his way of speaking of his " broken knees," or wrists, or ankles; for, despite his splendid physique— big chest and shoulders and limbs—his hands and feet are small, and his small-boned frame has ill withstood the severe strain put upon it in his youth, on sea and plain, river and lake and mountain—to say nothing of railroad, in his tramping days. Consequently, he cannot tie himself into convenient knots or roll into bundles as can I, and an hour on floor or ground, no matter how cushioned with banana and coco-nut-leaves, where he must sit cramp-legged, or crouch, is little short of agonizing.

And the luau ! At every place was a heap of food so attractive that one did not know which mysterious packet to open first. Each *had at least a quart of poi, of the approved royal-pink tint, in a big shiny goblet carved from a coco-nut thinned and polished and scalloped around the brim, and this substance as usual formed the *pièce de resistance*. There are varying consistencies of poi. The " one-finger " poi is thick enough ᴛᴏ admit of a sufficient mouthful being twirled at one twirl upon the forefinger ; two-fingered poi is thinner, requiring two digits to carry the required portion. I do not know whether or not three-fingered poi is ever exceeded ; but if it is, I am sure no true Hawaiian or kama-aina would hesitate to apply his whole fist to it.

It appeared etiquette to sample every delicacy forthwith, rather than to finish any one or two until all had been tasted. And we depended solely upon our fingers in place of forks and spoons. A twirl of poi on the forefinger is conveyed neatly to the mouth, followed promptly by a pinch of salt salmon, for seasoning, or of hot roast fish or beef or fowl steaming in freshly open leaf-wrappings ; for this is the excellent way roast foods are prepared, then laid in the ground among heated stones, and covered with earth. Thus none of the essential flavour is liberated until the clean hot leaves of the ti-plant, or the canna in absence of the ti, are taken off at table.

There was also chicken stewed in coco-nut milk, sweet and tasty, and, for relishes, outlandish forms of sea-life, particularly the *opihis* (o-peé-hees), 'salt and savoury, which we think we might come to prefer to raw oysters. Mullet is eaten raw, cut in tempting little grey cubes and dusted with native coarse red salt ; but while Jack pronounced it one of his favourite articles of diet henceforth whenever obtainable, I could not quite make the experiment. I may in time acquire a liking for well-seasoned raw fish, which in all logic is less offensive to the mind than live raw oysters and razor-back clams ; but fairly certain am I that never shall I assimilate *ake* (ah-kay)—which is raw liver and chile peppers, and a pet dish here.

Some small clams, *alamihi*, were very good, but I moved askance at the pinkish round tidbits from squid-tentacles, although my lord and master smacked his lips over them and urged me on. I contented myself with little par-boiled crabs and lobsters.

One toothsome accompaniment to a Hawaiian meal is the *kukui*, or candlenut, the meat of which is baked and broken up fine, and mixed with native salt. Pinches of this relish are eaten with poi and other viands, and it is sometimes stirred to season a mess of raw mullet. The kukui tree, a comparatively recent introduction from the South Seas, has nearly as many uses as the coco-nut palm, for aside from the gustatory excellence of its nut, a gum from the bark is valuable, and a dye found in the shell of the nut was formerly used to paint the intricate patterns of the tapa that served for clothing. This dye also formed a good waterproofing for tapa cloaks, and with it tattoo-artists drew fashionable designs into the flesh of their patrons, who also rubbed their bodies with oil pressed from the nut, especially for making them slippery for wrestling and fighting.

For the drinking there was choice of a mild beer and " pop " (soda-water of many colours), and coco-nut-water in the shell ; and for dessert, the not unpleasant anti-climax of good old vanilla ice-cream to remind us that Hawaii has long been in the grasp of Jack's " inevitable white man."

And then the dancing. Mr. Moore had promised us a *hula :* but a hula, except by professional dancers, is more easily promised than delivered. The native must be in the precise right humour of acquiescence before any performance is forthcoming for the malihini. Our pleasant task was to overcome the panicky shyness that whelmed both men and wahines when we coaxed them to show their paces. Few, very likely, had ever

danced before strangers. Indeed, for the most
part, the hula is forbidden by law. And the
majority of these were simple rural folk with a
terror of possible wrong-doing. I think the
Hawaiians are quick to detect a meretricious
gaiety or any patronizing overdone familiarity ;
and to make them feel one's genuine interest in
their customs is the only means by which to
establish a basis of social intercourse. Left to
themselves, they will dance anywhere at any
time. Tochigi witnessed his first hula on Tony's
train ! He did not comment upon it ; but after
seeing Americans dance, each couple following its
own method, he respectfully observed that he
thought we danced more for our own pleasure
than for that of onlookers !

At length a bolder or more persuadable spirit,
yearning to express the real general desire to
please, broke through the crust of reserve, and
began a series of body convolutions to the endless
two-step measure of guitars and ukuleles that
had throbbed in a leafy corner of the grass-shelter
during the luau.

Arch faces lighted up, hands clapped and feet
kept time, eyes and teeth flashed in the dim light
of lanterns and lamps, and flower-burdened
shoulders swung involuntarily to the irresistible
rhythm. One after another added the music
of his throat to an old hula that has never seen
printer's ink, while the violin threnody of the
Alapai raised the plaintive, half-savage lilt to
something incommunicably high and haunting.

Jack seemed in a trance, his eyes like stars, while his broad shoulders swayed to the measure. Discovering my regard, caught in his emotion of delight in this pregnant folk-dance and song, he did not smile, but half-veiled his eyes as he laid a hand on mine in token of acknowledgment of my comprehension of his deep mood. For in every manifestation of human life, he goes down into the tie-ribs of racial development, as if in eternal quest to connect up the abysmal past with the palpable present.

A pause, full of murmurs and low laughter, then a strapping young wahine with the profile of Diana seized an old guitar, and with a shout to another girl to get on her feet, leaned over and swept the strings masterfully with the backs of her fingers, at the same time setting up a wild, wanton, thrilling hula-song that was a love cry in the starlight, each repeated phrase ending in a fainting, crooning, tremulous falsetto which trailed off into a vanishing wisp of sound. She could not sit quietly, but swung her body and lissom limbs in rhythm like a wild thing possessed, seeming to galvanize the dancers by sheer force of will, for one by one they sprang to the bidding of her voice and magnetic fingers, into the flickering light where they swayed and bent and undulated like mad sweet nymphs and fauns. Now and again a brown sprite separated from the moving group, and came to dance before the haole guests, the dance a provocation to join the revelry. Sometimes the love-appeal was unmis-

takable, accompanied by singing words we wotted
not of, but which were the cause of much good-
natured merriment from the others.   Then suddenly the performer would become impersonal
in face and gesture, and melt back into the weav-
ing group.

After a while the dancing lagged, and we felt
it was time for us to relieve these kind people of our
more or less restraining presence.   They had done
so much, and to wear out such welcome would
have been a crime against good heart and manners.

Having neglected to ask the obliging Tony to
wait his dummy for our returning, down the track
we footed, listening to small noises of the night,
among which could be detected the sighing of
water-buffalo, those grotesque grey shapes that
patiently toil by day in the rice-fields.

PEARL LOCHS,
Friday, June 14, 1907.

Eleven days after Jack's broiling at Waikiki,
yesterday the largest blisters began forming on his
scarlet limbs—rising and running into one another
until a combined blister would be a foot long.
His interest in the phenomenon helps him pass the
irritating hours.   I shall be happy indeed for
both our sakes when he is once more comfortable,
for his condition keeps me in a nervous shudder
of sympathy.   But time slips by very entertain-
ingly, with a heated rubber of cribbage mornings
after breakfast of papaia and coffee and hot
crabs which Jack, in a reclining chair on the ter-

race, watches his industrious fish-wife pull in from the jetty. Then we read aloud until worktime, just now having finished Brand Whitlock's *The Turn of the Balance*, and begun on a course of George Moore's novels.

At lunch to-day Miss Johnson introduced us to a girl friend from Maine, and it was a unique experience to sit in the hot-house air, gazing out upon the hot-house vegetation, the while we conversed in " down-east " colloquialisms, among other incidents recalling one when Jack and I, on our honeymoon, drove for the first time in a cab-on-runners over the crackling streets of Bangor after a freeze-up. " Did you see her jump at the sound of that falling leaf ? " Jack laughed on the way home, for the young lady from Maine was not the only one startled when a twenty-foot frond let go its parent palm and crashed to earth.

Our captain of the roseate name is painting the *Snark*, and she floats, a boat of white enamel, in the still blue and silver of the morning flood, while for frame to the fair picture a painted double rainbow over-arches, flinging the misty fringes of its ends in our enraptured faces. From the shell-pink dawn, through the green and golden day, to sunset and purple twilight and starshine, we move in beauty. " What a lot of people must have been shanghaied here by their own desire ! " Jack ruminates. And truly, Hawaii is sufficient excuse for never going home.

Mr. Scott, of the Iron Works, sailed over from

Honolulu last Sunday in his fast yacht, the
Kamehameha, and she was a lovely sight slanting
about on the crisp water in a fresh whiff of wind,
her owner doing some fancy sailing around the
Snark, apparently trying to see how close he could
sail without touching. With him came a corps
of engineers who had offered to give their holiday
for the fellow who wrote *The Game* and *The Sea
Wolf*. Jack was quite overwhelmed by this tribute,
to the shame of his own state and her lukewarm
workmen. He was especially pleased over the
liking of these young men for *The Game*, which is
a favourite of his own, few Americans seeming to
care for it, although England and her colonies
" eat it up."

Gene has coaxed our launch into action, and
in it we rode to the yacht. Jack is delighted,
for it has been useless ever since the time in
San Francisco when it was allowed to lie for
weeks full of salt water, well-nigh ruining the
little engine. While Jack talked business aboard,
I swam back alone to shore with the launch in
attendance. " I never thought I should marry a
woman who could swim like that ! " he shouted
after me. " You didn't," the woman puffed ;
" you taught her to swim like that ! " And
now we look forward to days when together we
shall swim for hours beyond the breakers at
Waikiki, and anywhere in the world.

Jack London is a devoted card-player who
seldom finds chance to sharpen his wits on a good
game ; but he finds sport these evenings in play-

ing four-handed hearts, or whist, with Martin, Gene, and myself. I am not at all talented in the direction of games ; but because of Jack's fondness for cards I make a supreme effort to be at least an average player, finding much enjoyment in the contest. There is pleasure and profit in almost anything one undertakes to learn of " the other fellow's game " in this world, if one but employs a little selfless understanding.

Last evening there were no cards, for we had opportunity again to come in contact with the Hawaiians, receiving a party in our sylvan drawing and music-room. Miss Johnson had told us that Judge Hookanu (Ho-o-kah-noo), the native district judge at Pearl City, wished to bring his wife to call. To our prompt invitation they responded with all the immediate family as well as more distant relatives. One of these, who dislikes Americans, during a conversation with Miss Johnson concerning the Londons, remarked : " Oh, yes, the English are always very nice." " But the Londons are American—very American ! " Miss Johnson straightened her out. However, the dusky lady was cordial enough when our meeting took place, as were all the party. The judge proved an intelligent and kindly soul, and Mrs. Hookanu, whom we have long admired at a distance, is a magnificently proportioned woman with the port of a queen, always attired in stately lines of black lawn or silk.

None of our visitors had heard the records of Hawaiian music which we played for them, and clapped their hands over the hulas like joyous children. But those merry hands folded meekly and devoutly when the Trinity Choir voices rose on the night air, and all joined in singing the harmonies of "Lead Kindly Light" and the several other beautiful hymns, especial favourites of my irreligious philosopher. The spirit of these folk is so sweet, so guileless. I know I shall love them for ever. Manners among them are gentle and considerate, so courteous in every conventional observance, prompted by their simple, affectionate hearts. Hookanu means *proud*, and these who bear the name demonstrate a blending of pride and gentlehood that is altogether aristocratic.

While Jack manipulated the talking-machine, I lay happily with head in a friendly lap while satin brown fingers caressed face and hair, looking high through the lacy foliage to where big stars hung like bright fruit in the branches. Jack wound up with the Hawaiian National Anthem, and the judge removed his hat and stood, the others rising about him. Then we cajoled them into contributing their own music, and after some hesitation, untinged by the faintest unwillingness, they settled dreamily to singing their favourite melodies—brown-velvet maids with laughing, shining eyes, who warbled in voices thin and penetrating as sweet zither-strings, softly, as if afraid to vex the calm night with greater volume.

At parting we walked to the gate, arms around the willing shoulders of our new friends, their

own " Aloha nui " on our lips. And every aloha
spoken or sung in Hawaii is the tender tone-
fall of a dying bell, tolling for the old Hawaii
Nei.

Then, arms-around, we two paced back across
the grass, and stood for a moment on the edge
of our bewitching garden, looking at the slender
sliver of a new moon of good omen dipping low
above the shadowy hills.

WAIKIKI,
Tuesday, June 25, 1907.

Once more in the brown tent-cottage at Waikiki,
as the hub for many spokes of exploration in
the islands. I mistrust we shall never again
pursue our idyllic life at the peninsula. Unfortunately, no way has been devised to live in two
or more places simultaneously—except in the
imagination, and that we can richly do.

Many jaunts are in the air : an automobile
journey around Oahu ; a yacht-race girdling
the same island, on which " Wahine Kapu," no
woman, is writ large upon the visages of the yachts-
men ; a torchlight fishing expedition fifty miles
distant with Prince " Cupid," under the same
rules ; a wonderful trip to Maui, to camp through
the greatest extinct crater in the world, Haleakala,
said to surpass Etna in extent and elevation ;
and Jack has been deftly pulling wires to bring
about a visit for us both to the famous Leper
Settlement on Molokai, which we hear occupies
one of the most beautiful sites in the islands.

Lucius E. Pinkham, President of the Board of Health, has been our guest to dinner, and not only has he put no obstacles in our way, but seems anxious for us to see Molokai. There has been considerable misrepresentation of the Settlement, and he evidently believes that Jack will write a fair picture. Mr. Pinkham seems to have the welfare of the lepers close at heart ; and I have heard that when he fails to obtain from the Government certain appropriations for improvements, he draws on his own funds.

Thus, the air is brimful of glamour and excitement, which helps to offset a tender regret for the lovely lochs and for our neighbours who have been so lavish in neighbourliness. One night before we departed, the Hookanu young folk arranged a crabbing party, and sang the hours away under the light of a half-moon ; another time, at sunset, we fished off Mr. Schwank's premises on the lee shore of the peninsula, where we landed a mess of " coloured fish " like a flock of wet butterflies. On his own soil we found our lusty ship carpenter most cordial, plying us with fruit and coco-nuts, and laughing with childlike joy at our praise of his tiny farm garden, and bridling with pride over our admiration of his handsome Portuguese wife and their children.

Here at the beach life is so gay there is hardly time to sleep and work, what with arrivals of transports and their ensuing dinners and dances in the hotel lanai, swimming and surf-boarding under sun and moon—very circumspectly under the sun ! One fine day we essayed to ride the breakers in a Canadian canoe, and capsized in a wild smother exactly as we had been warned. I stayed under water such a time that Jack, alarmed, came hunting for me ; but I was safe beneath the overturned canoe, which I was holding from bumping my head. He was so relieved to find me unhurt and capable of staying submerged so long that promptly he read me a lecture upon swimming as fast as possible from a capsized boat, to avoid being struck in event of succeeding rollers flinging it about.

One night, with Mr. and Mrs. Hawes, we attended a moonlight swimming party at the seaside home of Mr. and Mrs. C. Hedemann, long-time Danish residents of Honolulu, and became acquainted with more of the white islands' people. A lovely custom prevails here among the owners, who, in absences abroad, allow friends the use of their suburban places for occasions of this kind. Across the hedges we peeped into the next garden, where Robert Louis Stevenson lived during his visit to Honolulu.

After a military dance at the hotel last evening, tables were carried out on the lawn to the sand's edge, where a supper was served by silent swift Japanese in white. It was like a dream, sitting there among the trees hung with soft rosy lights, our eyes sweeping the horizon touched by a low golden moon, and across the effervescing foam of an ebbing tide at our feet, and the white seahorses charging the crescent beach, to Diamond

Head   purple-black   against   the   star-dusted
southern sky.   " Do you know where you are ? "
And there was but one answer to Jack's whisper—
" Just Waikiki," which tells it all.   The charm
of Waikiki—it is the charm of Hawaii Nei,
" All Hawaii."

WAIKIKI,
Friday, June 28, 1907.

To Mr. Ford we owe a new debt of gratitude.
And so does Hawaii, for such another promoter
never existed.   All he does is for Hawaii, desiring
nothing for himself except the feverish unremit-
ting pleasure of sharing the attractions of his
adopted land.   The past two days have been
spent encircling Oahu, or partly so, since only
the railroad continues around the entire shore-
line, the automobile drive cutting across a table-
land midway of the island.   Oahu comprises an
area of 598 square miles, is trapezoidal in shape,
and its coast is the most regular of any in the
group.   Another notable feature is that it possesses two distinct mountain chains, Koolau and
Waianae, whereas the other islands have isolated
peaks and no distinct ranges.   Waianae is much
the older of the two.   The geology of this volcanic
isle is a continual temptation to diverge.

The two machines carried ten of us, including
the drivers, two young fellows who, it was plain
to see, hung upon every word of Jack—oyster
pirate, tramp, war correspondent, and what not.
The party was composed of men whom Mr. Ford
wanted Jack to know, representing the best

of Hawaii's white citizenship. There was Mr. Joseph P. Cook, dominating figure of Alexander & Baldwin, which firm is the leading financial force of the islands. (It was Mr. Cook's missionary grandparents, the Amos P. Cooks, who founded, and for many years conducted, what was known as the " Chiefs' School," afterward called the " Royal School," which was patronized by all of the higher chiefs and their families). Mr. Lorrin A. Thurston, descended from the first missionaries, and associated conspicuously with the affairs of Hawaii, both monarchical and republican—and incidentally owner of the morning paper of Honolulu ; and Senor A. de Souza Canovarro, Portuguese Consul, an able man who has lived here twenty years and whose brain is shelved with islands' lore.

The world was all dewy cool and the air redolent with flowers when, after our early dip in the surf, we glided down Kalakaua Avenue between the awakening duck-ponds with their lily-pads and grassy partitions. Leaving the centre of town by way of Nuuanu Avenue, along which an electric car runs for two miles, we headed for the storied heights of the Pali (precipice), and presently began climbing toward the converging walls to the pass through the Koolau Range. This Nuuanu Valley is a wondrous residence section, of old-fashioned white mansions of bygone styles of architecture, still wearing their stateliness like a page in history. The dwellers therein are cooled by every breeze—not to mention

frequent rains. It is a humorous custom for a
resident to say, " I live at the first shower," or
the second shower, or even the third, according
to his distance from wetter elevations in the city
limits. The rainfall in Nuuanu, and Manoa,
the next valley to the south-east, is from 140
inches to 150 inches annually. Many of these
old houses stand amidst expansive lawns, the
drive-ways columned with royal palms—the
first brought to the islands. One white New
England house was pointed out as the country
home of Queen Emma, bought with its adjoining
acres by the Government and turned into a
public park. The old building contains some of
the Queen's furniture, and other antiques of the
period. " The Daughters of Hawaii," an organ-
ization of Hawaii-born women of all nationalities,
has the care of the whole premises.

I promised myself an afternoon in the cemetery,
where quaint tombs show through the beautiful
trees and shrubbery, and where, in the mausoleum, are laid the bones of the Kamehameha
and Kalakaua dynasties. King Lunalilo, who
succeeded the last of the Kamehamehas and
preceded Kalakaua, rests in the mausoleum of
Kawaiahoa Church in town.

Up we swung on a smooth road graded along
the hill-sides, the sides of the valley gradually
drawing together, the violet-shadowed walls of
the mountains growing more sheer until they
seemed almost to overtop with their clouded
heads breaking into morning gold—Lanihuli and

Konahuanui rising 3000 feet to left and right. From a keen curve, we looked back and down the green miles we had come, to a fairy-white city lying suffused in blue mist beside a fairy-blue sea.

Four miles from the end of the car-track, quite unexpectedly to me, suddenly the machine emerged from a narrow defile upon a platform hewn out of the rocky earth, and my senses were momentarily stunned, for it seemed that the island had broken off, fallen away beneath our feet to the east. On foot, pressing against a wall of wind that eternally draughts through the pass, and threading among a dozen small pack-mules resting on the way to Honolulu, we gained the railed brink of the Pali. To the centre of a scene that has haunted me for years, since I beheld it in a painting at the Pan-American Exposition at Buffalo, I looked down 1000 feet into an emerald abyss over the awful pitch of which Kamehameha a century ago forced the warriors of the King of Oahu, Kalanikupule— a " legion of the lost ones " whose shining skulls became souvenirs for strong climbers in succeeding generations. Some one pointed to a ferny, bowery spot far below, where Prince Cupid once kept a hunting cabin ; but there was now no trace of it or of any trail penetrating the dense jungle.

To the left, lying north-west, stretch the per-pendicular, inaccessible ramparts of the Koolau Range which extends the length of the island, bastioned by erosions, and based in rich green slopes of forest and pasture that fall away to alluvial plains fertile with rice and cane, and rippled with green hillocks. Where we stood, an offshoot of the range bent in a right-angle to the eastward at our back ; and off to the right, the great valley is bounded by desultory low hills, amid which an alluring red road leads to Kailua and Waimanalo by the sapphire sea, where we are told the bathing beaches are wonderful.

A reef-embraced bay on the white-fringed shore caused me to inquire why Honolulu had not been builded upon this cool windward coast of Oahu, with its opulent and ready-made soil. " Any navigator could tell you that," Jack chided. " Honolulu was begun when there was no steam, and the lee side of the island was the only safe anchorage for sailing vessels."

The sun was now burning up the moving mists below, and through the opalescent rents and thinning spaces we could trace the ruddy ribbon of road we were to travel. If I had dreamed of the majestic grandeur of these mountains, of the wondrous painted valley to the east, how feebly I should have anticipated other islands until first learning this one. Jack keeps repeating that he cannot understand why it is not thronged with tourists, and calls it the garden of the world. We have seen nothing like it in America or Europe. And yet Oahu is not spoken of as by any means the most beautiful of the Hawaiian Islands. Instead, both residents and visitors rave over the

" Garden Isle," Kauai, the Kona Coast of Hawaii
and that Big Island's gulches, the wonders of
Maui with its Iao Valley and Haleakala, " The
House of the Sun." What must they all be, say
we, if these persons have not been stirred by
Windward Oahu !

After clinging spellbound to our windy vantage
for half an hour (Jack meanwhile not forgetting
to calculate how many times Kalanikupule's
unfortunate army bumped in its headlong fall),
we coasted the intricate curves of a road that is
railed and reinforced with masonry, fairly hanging to a stark wall for the best part of two miles.
I noticed that Mr. Cook preferred himself to
negotiate his White Steamer on this blood-
tingling descent, until we rounded into the
undulating floor of the plain, where we stared
abruptly up at the astonishing way we had come,
with its retaining walls of cement, some of them
400 feet in length.

One stands at the base of an uncompromising
two-thousand-foot crag, an outjut of the range,
and it appears but a few hundred feet to its head.
Everything is as if seen in a mirror that has been
dulled by a silver breath. That is it—it is all a
reflection—these are mirrored mountains and
shall always remain to me like something en-
visioned in a glass. " Do you know where you
are ? " But I shook my head and hand to Jack's
amused call. Never did I imagine Oahu was
like this on its other side.

I for one was commencing to realize how early

I had breakfasted, when we turned aside from the road on which we had been running through miles of the Kahuku Sugar Plantation, into a private drive-way that led to Mrs. James B. Castle's sea-rim retreat, The Dunes.   Having been called un-expectedly to Honolulu, she had left the manager of the plantation, Mr. Andrew Adams, to do the honours, together with a note of apology embody-ing the wish that we make ourselves at home, and a request that we write in her guest-book. After luncheon the men insisted that I inscribe something fitting for them to witness.   Warm and tired and dull, I wrote the following unin-spired if grateful sentiment :—

" With appreciation of the perfect hospitality— and deep regret that the giver was absent."

The others followed with their signatures; and when Mr. Ford's turn came his eye read what I had written, but his unresting mind must have been wool-gathering, for he scribbled :—

" Hoping that every passer-by may be as fortunate."

A chorus of derision caused him to bend an alarmed eye upon the page, which he carefully scanned, especially my latter phrase.   And then out came the page.   Mr. Cook unavailingly assured him that Mrs. Castle enjoyed a good joke, but the scarlet-faced Ford was not to be induced to replace the sheet.   I then prepared another, to which our friend affixed his autograph.   This is the first time we have ever seen that irrepressible gentleman crestfallen in the least degree ; and he remained subdued for the rest of the day. " Man, man, why don't you relax once in a while ? " I had said to him earlier in the day, " You'll wear yourself out before you're forty. You should dwell at length upon words like Eternity, Repose, Rome——" but I was interrupted by " Oh, fudge ! " as he saw what difficulty I was having to preserve a grave countenance.

Mr. Adams showed us over the labour barracks —neat settlements of Japanese and Portuguese in which he seems deeply interested, especially as concerns the future of the younger element— the swarms of beautiful children that we saw rolling in the grass. The Portuguese flocked around the consul, who was apparently an old and loved friend.

Several miles farther, we came to the Reform School, where the erring youth of Oahu are guided in the way they should go by Mr. Gibson, a keen-faced, wiry man who has made splendid showing with the boys, who are largely of the native stock. There was not a criminal face among them, and probably the majority are detained for temperamental laxness of one sort or other. Emotional they are, and easily led, and inordinately fond of games of chance—but dishonest, never. A small sugar plantation is carried on in connection with the school, which is worked by the boys.

Our last lap was the Reform School to Waialua,

F

which lies at the sea edge of the Waialua Plantation. *Haleiwa* means " House Beautiful," and is
pronounced Hah-lay-e-vah. There is so much
dissension as to how the " v " sound crept into
the " w," that I am going to keep out of it, and
retire with the statement that Alexander, in his
splendid *History of the Hawaiian People*, remarks,
" The. letter ' w.' generally sounds like ' v '
between the penult and final syllable of a word."

House and grounds are very attractive, broad
lawns sloping to an estuary just inside the beach,
and in this river-like bit of water picturesque
fishing boats and canoes lie at anchor. A span
of rustic Japanese bridge leads to the bath-
houses, and here we went for a swim before dinner.
We would not advise beginners to choose this
beach for their first swimming lessons, for it
shelves with startling abruptness, while the
undertow is more noticeable than at Waikiki.
But for those who can take care of themselves,
this lively water is good sport and more bracing
than on the leeward coast.

We strolled through the gardens and along
green little dams between duck-ponds spotted
with lily-pads, and the men renewed their boyhood by " chucking " rocks into a sumptuous
mango tree, bringing down the russet-gold fruit
for an appetizer. I may some day be rash enough
to describe the flavour of a mango, or try to ; but
not yet—although I seem to resent some author's
statement that it bears a trace of turpentine.

Leaving Haleiwa next morning, we deserted the

seashore for very different country. For a while
the motor ascended steadily toward the south-
west, on a fine red road—so red that on ahead
the very atmosphere was rose-tinted. Looking
back as we climbed, many a lovely surf-picture
rewarded the quest of our eyes, white breakers
ruffling the crescent beaches, with a sea bluer than
the deep blue sky.

At an elevation of about 800 feet we struck the
rolling green prairie-land of the " Plains," where
the ocean is visible north-west and south-east, on
both sides of the island. Such a wonderful
table-land, between mountain walls, swept by the
freshening north-east trade-wind—miles upon
miles of rich grazing, and hill upon hill ruled with
blue-green lines of pineapple growth. At one
pineapple plantation we stopped that Jack might
take a look around at the fabulously promising
industry. Mr. Kellogg, the manager, gave an
interesting demonstration of how simple is the
cultivation of the luscious " pines," and held
stoutly that a woman, unaided, could earn a good
living out of a fair patch. " So you see, my dear,"
Jack advised me, " when I can't write any longer,
you can keep both of us at Wahiawa ! "

Like prairie seen from a distance, we discovered
that this section of Oahu is serrated in some portions by enormous gullies, in character resembling ·
our California barrancas, but of vastly greater
proportions A great dam has been constructed
for the purpose of conserving the water for irrigation.

Something went wrong with Mr. Cook's machine, and he was obliged to telephone from Wahiawa to Honolulu for some fixtures. Think of this old savage isle in the middle of the Pacific Ocean, where, from its high interior, one may talk over a wire to a modern city for modern parts of a " horseless carriage," to be sent by steam over a steel track ! It is stimulating once in a day to ponder the age in which we live.

WAIKIKI,
June 29, 1907.

" Have you seen the Cleghorn Gardens ? " is a frequent question to the malihini, and only another way of asking if one has seen the gardens of the late Princess Victoria Kaiulani, lovely hybrid flower of Scottish and Polynesian parentage, daughter of a princess of Hawaii, Miriam Likelike (sister of Liliuokalani and Kalakaua) and the Honourable Arthur Scott Cleghorn. We are too late by twenty years to be welcomed by Likelike, and eight years behind time to hear the merriment of Kaiulani in her father's house— Kaiulani, who would now be of the same age as Jack London. King Kalakaua died at the Palace Hotel in San Francisco on January 20, 1891, and when his remains arrived in Honolulu from the U.S.S. Charlestown nine days later, and his sister Liliuokalani was proclaimed his successor, the little Princess Kaiulani, their niece, was appointed heir-apparent. And now her venerable father's acquaintance we have added to our vital impressions of Hawaii.

The famous house, Ainahau, is not visible from the avenue. Here the bereft consort of Like-like lives in solitary state with his servants, amid the relics of unforgotten days. He receives few visitors, and we felt as if breaking his privacy were an intrusion, even though by invitation. But the commandingly tall, courtly old Scot, wide brown eyes smiling benevolently under white hair and beetling brows, paced half-way down his palm-pillared drive-way in greeting, and led our little party about the green-shady ways of the wonderland of flowers and vines, lily-ponds and arbours, " Where Kaiulani sat," or sewed, or read, or entertained—all in a forest of high interlacing trees of many varieties, both native and foreign. I was most fascinated by a splendid banyan, a tree which from childhood I had wanted to see. This pleased the owner, whose especial pride it is—" Kaiulani's banyan " ; although he is obliged to trim it unmercifully lest its predatory tentacles capture the entire park.

Into nurseries and vegetable gardens we followed him, and real grass huts that have stood untouched for years. Another pride of Mr. Cleghorn's is his sixteen varieties of hibiscus, of sizes and shapes and tints that we would hardly have believed possible—magic puffs of exquisite colour springing like miracles from slender green stems that are often too slight for the blooms, and snap under the full blossom-weight.

And the house. The portion once occupied by the vanished princess is never opened to strangers, nor used in any way. Only her father wanders there, investing the pretty suite of rooms with recollection of her tuneful young presence. For she was little over twenty when she died.

But in the great drawing-room we were made welcome, reached by three broad descending steps, and containing works of art and curios from all the world ; old furniture from European palaces that would be the despair of a repulsed collector ; tables of lustrous Hawaiian woods fashioned to order in Germany half a century ago ; rare Oriental vases set upon flare-topped pedestals ingeniously made from inverted tree-stumps of beautiful brown *kou* wood, polished like marble ; a quaint and stately concert grand piano ; and, .most fascinating of all, treasures of Hawaiian courts, among them some of the marvellous feather work. In the dim corners of the immense room, *kahilis* stand as if on guard—barbaric royal insignia, plumed staffs of state, some of them twice the height of a man. The feathers are fastened at right angles to the pole of shining hardwood, forming a barrel-shaped decoration, somewhat like our hearse-plumes of a past generation. But the kahili is only some-times of funeral hue, more often flaming in scarlet, or some grade of the rich yellows loved of the islanders. Originally a fly-brush in savage courts, the kahili progressed in dignity through the dyn-asties to an indispensable adjunct to official occa-sions, sometimes exceeding thirty feet in height. To me, it and the outrigger canoe are the most significantly impressive and splendid of royal barbaric forms.

The walls of the room are solidly ranged with books for some two-thirds of their height, and above the books hang fascinating old portraits of bygone Hawaiian royalty as well as famous personages of the outer world. Jack's eyes snapped as he fingered the old volumes—I can see his face now, avid as always to read every word between the covers of every book ever made by man. Not because these were rare old editions in rare old bindings was he wooed, but just because they were books, old books with their chronicles of the minds and hearts, hazards and achievements of mankind.

Francesca Colonna Hawes, with whom we had come, opened her incredible black eyes in astonishment, the while we sat at tea in a narrow red-tiled room overlooking a court of flowers, when our host remarked in his grave voice :—

" Why can you not write in my gardens, Mr. London ? It would please me. You are very welcome to come every day. And you would be entirely undisturbed. Why not, now ? "

According to Mrs. Hawes, this is an unheard-of consideration in these times of Mr. Cleghorn's seclusion. " Why don't you ? " I queried of Jack, on the way home. " Maybe I shall," he replied. But I think he will not, for he is curiously timorous about availing himself of favours.

Mr. Cleghorn also suggested that he could arrange a private audience with Queen Liliuokalani

at her residence in town, if we desired.   Which
reminds me that Jack holds a letter of introduction to her from Charles Warren Stoddard, who
knew her in the days of her tempestuous reign.
He and Jack have called each other Dad and Son
for years, although acquainted only by corres-
pondence.   But we have little wish to intrude
upon the Queen, for it can be scant pleasure to
her to meet Americans, no matter how sympathetic
they may be with her changed state.

 ·Upon a carven desk lay open a guest-book, an
old ledger, in which we were asked to leave our
hand.   The first name written in this thick tome
is that of " Oskar, of Sweden and Norway," and,
running over the fascinating yellowed pages,
among other notable autographs we read that of
Agassiz.

Here, there, and everywhere, in photograph,
in oil portraiture, on wall and upon easel, we met
the lovely, pale face of the bereft old father's
daughter, Kaiulani, in whose memory he seems
to exist in a mood of adoration.   Every event
dates from her untimely passing.   " When
Kaiulani died," he would begin ; or " Since
Kaiulani went away," and " Before Kaiulani left
me——" was the burden of his thought and conversation concerning the past of which we loved
to hear.   Pictures show her to have been a
woman possessing the beauty of both races,
proud, loving, sensitive, spirituelle, with the
characteristic curling mouth and great luminous
brown eyes of the Hawaiian, looking out wist-

fully upon a world of pleasure and opportunity that could not detain her frail body. Flower of romance she was—romance that nothing in the old books of South Sea adventuring can rival; her sire, a handsome roving boy ashore from an English ship back in the '50's; her mother, a dusky princess of the blood royal, who loved the handsome white-skinned youth and constituted him Governor of Oahu under the Crown, that she might with honour espouse him.

And now, the boy, grown old—his Caucasian vitality having survived the gentle Polynesian blood of the wife who brought him laurels in her own land—having watched the changing administrations of that land and race for nearly three score years, abides alone with the shadow of her and of the pale daughter with the poet brow who did honour to them both by coming into being. To this winsome child-woman, previous to her voyage to England's Court, Robert Louis Stevenson, living where we peeped into the garden but a few nights gone, sent the following :—

[Written in April to Kaiulani in the April of her age ; and at Waikiki, within easy walk of Kaiulani's banyan ! When she comes to my land and her father's, and the rain beats upon the window (as I fear it will), let her look at this page ; it will be like a weed gathered and pressed at home ; and she will remember her own islands, and the shadow of the mighty tree ; and she will hear the peacocks screaming in the dusk and the wind blowing in the palms ; and she will think of her father sitting there alone.—R. L. S.]

" Forth from her land to mine she goes,
The island maid, the island rose,
Light of heart and bright of face :
The daughter of a double race.

Her islands here, in Southern sun,
Shall mourn their Kaiulani gone ;
And I in her dear banyan shade,
Look vainly for my little maid.

But our Scots islands far away
Shall glitter with unwonted day,
And cast for once their tempests by
To smile in Kaiulani's eye."

ABOARD THE NOEAU, BOUND FOR MOLOKAI,
Monday Evening, July 1, 1907.

" *Noeau* " (No-a-ah-oo—quickly No-a-ow)—
the very name has a mournful, ominous sound ;
Noeau, ship of despair, ferry of human freight
condemned.   We are not merry, Jack and I, for
what we have witnessed during the past two hours
would wring pitying emotion from a graven image.
And just when we would cheer a trifle, it not
being our mutual temperament long to remain
downcast, our eyes are again compelled by the
huddle of doomed fellow-creatures amidst their
pathetic bundles of belongings on the open after-
deck of the plunging interisland steamer bound
for Molokai.

None of it did we miss—the parting and the
embarkation of the banished ; and never, should
I live a thousand fair years, shall I forget the
memory of that strange, rending, wailing, escaping

bestiality by its very deliberateness, for, no matter how deep and true may be the grief, this wailing expression of it constitutes a ceremonial in this as in other countries where it survives as a set form of lamentation. Shrill, piercing, it curdled the primitive life-current in us, every tone in the gamut of sorrow being played upon the plaintive word *auwe* (ah-oo-way'—quickly ow-way'), *alas*, in recurrent chorusing when each parting took place and the loved one stepped upon the gang-plank, untouched by the officers and crew of the small steamer.

" Clean " passengers were taken aboard first, the vessel picking up at another wharf those who bore no return ticket to the land of the clean. As the *Noeau* came alongside, the crowd ashore appeared like any other leave-taking gathering of natives, even to the flowers ; but suddenly Jack at my elbow jerked out, " *Loo*ᴋ—look at that boy's face ! " And I looked, and saw. It was a lad of twelve or so, and one of his cheeks was so swollen that the bursting eye seemed as if extended on a fleshy horn—a horrible sight. Beside him a woman hovered, her face dark with sorrow. Our eyes were soon quick to detect the marks and roved from face to face, selecting fairly accurately those who proved later to be passengers for the dark fifty-odd miles across Kaiwi Channel and along the north coast of Molokai to the village of Kalaupapa that is their final destina-tion and home on this earth.

But one can only see what one can see, and

there were men and women among these who bore no apparent blemish ; and yet, this moment we can distinguish these among the disfigured company on the lurching after-deck.

The ultimate wrench of hearts and hands, the supreme acme of ruth, came when, separated by the widening breach between steamer and dock, the lost and the deserted gazed for the last time upon one another, and the last pitiful offerings of leis fell into the water. No normal malihini could stand by untouched ; it was so utterly, hopelessly sad—a funeral in which the dead themselves walked.

For one white child, a blonde-haired little German maid, we felt especial solicitude. Her bronze companions all had dear ones to wail for them and for whom to " keen." But she stood quite apart, with dry eyes old before their time, watching an alien race deliver its woe in ways she had not learned. Whose baby is she ? To whom is she dear ? Where is the mother who bore her ? And the answer was just now volunteered by the Superintendent of the Leper Colony, returning from a vacation, Mr. J. D. McVeigh. The child's mother is already in Kalaupapa, far gone with a rapid form of leprosy ; and this little daughter, who had been left with a drunken father who treated her ill, has been found with the same form, and will live but a few years. So she is going to her own, and her own is waiting for her, and it is well. But think of the whole distorted face of the dream of life—dear Christ !

. . . Now the white child has fallen asleep in a dull red sunset glow, her flaxen head in the lap of a beautiful hapa haole girl who carries no apparent spot of corrosion. She looks down right motherly upon the tired face of the small Saxon maid. Hawaiian women eternally " rock cradles in their hearts," which are so expansive that it is said to matter little whose child they cradle—bringing up one another's offspring with impartial loving-kindness. This practice extended even into highest circles, as Queen Liliuokalani attests in her own entertaining book, *Hawaii's Story by Hawaii's Queen*. She herself was " given away " at birth, wrapped in the finest tapacloth, to Konia, a granddaughter of Kamehameha the Great, wedded to a high chief, Paki. Their own daughter, Bernice Pauahi, Liliuokalani's foster-sister, was afterward married to C. R. Bishop, Minister of Foreign Affairs in 1893 under King Lunalilo, Kalakaua's predecessor. The Queen writes that in using the term foster-sister she merely adopts one customary in the English language, there being no such modification recognized in her own tongue. As a matter of fact, in childhood she knew no other parents than Paki and Konia, no other sister than Pauahi. Her own father and mother were no more than interesting acquaintances. For this custom she offers only the reason that the alliance by adoption cemented ties of friendship between chiefs, which, spreading to the common people, doubtless encouraged harmony—a harmony that would have delighted King Solomon, to say nothing of white men's courts of law !

They forget quickly, these Hawaiians, one hears ; and one must believe, I suppose—and, believing, thank whatever gods may be, for this blissful latitude never was created for the harbouring of grief. But the ability or tendency to forget pain has little to do with its momentary poignancy. The sun-warm Hawaiian suffers with all the abandon of the blood that keeps him always young. The sorrow is real, and the weeping. If these people could not recover speedily from despair, they would die off faster than they are already perishing from their Arcadian isles.

On our deck, observing the dolorous scene aft, is a young native girl, round and ripe and more lovely than any we have yet seen. Clean and wholesome, unsullied by any blight, a happy body, she stands beside her father, a handsome grey-haired Hawaiian with lofty mien ; and one wonders what are the young girl's thoughts as she gazes upon these wrecks of her kind. And yet, she herself might have to be sought in Molokai another year. As well seek her underground, is the next thought. Poor human flesh and blood !

KALAUPAPA, MOLOKAI,
Tuesday, July 2, 1907.

We are endeavouring to reconstruct whatever mind-picture we have hitherto entertained of that grave of living death, Molokai. But it is no use, and we might as well give it up. Eye and brain are possessed of the bewildering actuality, and having expected heaven knows what lugubrious prospect, we are all at sea. Certain it is that all preconceptions were far removed from the joyous sunny scene now before us, as I rock in a hammock on the Superintendent's lanai, shaded from the late sunshine by a starry screen of white jasmine. Jack stretches at length on a rattan lounge, cigarette in one hand and long cool glass in the other; and what we see is a peaceful pasture of many acres, a sort of bulging village green, in the centre a white band-stand breathing of festivity. Around the verdant semi-hemisphere, widely straggling as if space and real estate values were the least consideration of mankind, dot the flower-bedecked homes of the leprous inhabitants. Breaking rudely into this vision of infinite repose, a cowboy on a black horse dashes furiously across the field and whirls out of sight. A leper. Two comely wahines in ruffly white holokus, starched to a nicety, stroll chatting by the house, looking up brightly to smile Aloha with eyes and lips. Lepers. Jack looks at me. I look at Jack. And this is Molokai the dread; Molokai, isle of despair, where Father Damien spent his martyrdom.

The Settlement lies on a triangle, a sort of wide-based peninsula, shut effectively off from the rest of the island to the south by a formidable wall rising 4000 feet into the deep blue sky—a wall of mystery, for it is well nigh unscalable except by the bands of wild goats that we can discover only by aid of Mr. McVeigh's telescope. Every little while, as a sailor sweeps the horizon, he steps to the glass, hidden from the community by the jasmine screen, and studies the land of his charge, keeping track of the doings of the village.

The only trail out of or into this isolated lowland zigzags the bare face of the pali near its northern end, at the seagirt extremity of the Settlement reserve. A silvery-green cluster of kukui trees marks the beginning of the trail not far up from the water's edge. Thus far and no farther may the residents of the peninsula stray; and the telescope is most often trained to this point of the compass. That trail does not look over-inviting; but we have set our hearts upon leaving Kalaupapa by this route, albeit Mr. McVeigh, who kens what is in our thought, warns us that it is undergoing repairs and is unsafe. Indeed, he has gone so far as to say that it is out of the question for us to ascend it in its present dilapidated condition.

In view of the pleasant reality of the island, yesternight's racking experience seems a nightmare. Over and above pity for the stricken exiles, we were none too comfortable ourselves, for in the tiny stuffy staterooms it was impossible to sleep, and except for coolness the populous deck was scarcely less disturbing. Besides the Superintendent, the other passengers were hapa-haoles and a white Catholic Father with his Bishop, bound for the Settlement to inspect their institutions.

We turned in early on deck-mattresses, after listening to some thrilling yarns from the captain and mate of the sorry little steamer, to say nothing of those of Mr. McVeigh, who sparkles with Hibernian wit. As the miles and time increased between the lepers and the harbour of farewells, they searched out their ubiquitous ukuleles and guitars, and rendered us all happier for their presence, poor things. All would have been well, and the music and murmuring voices soon have had us drowsing, but for a tipsy native sailor who chipped in noisily with ribald song and speech that was loudly profane.

At frequent intervals the captain and mates issued from their unrestful cubbies on the short strip of plunging deck (these interisland channels have a reputation equal to the passage between Dover and Calais), and conversed at length in unmuffled accents. To cap my sleepless discomfort, Jack, who had been fighting all night, he avers unconsciously, to wrest away the soft pillow he had insisted upon my using, finally appropriated the same with a determined ' pounding of the ear '' in hobo parlance. And poor I, lacking the meanness to reclaim it at price of rousing the tender soul from his troubled slumber, languished upon a neck-wrenching bolster stuffed, I swear, with scrap-iron. It has since occurred to us that it may have been a life-preserver.

At the dim chill hour of four, all passengers for Kalaupapa were landed in a rough-and-ready lifeboat through breakers which, to our regret, were the reverse of boisterous. We had looked forward to making through a breach of surf like that shown in photographs of Kalaupapa Landing. But it was novel enough, this being let down the lurching black flank of the ship where she rolled in the unseen swell, into an uncertain boat where muscular arms eased us into invisible seats. The merest fitful whisper of air was stirring, and there was something solemn in our progress, deep-dipping oars sending the heavy boat in large slow rhythm over a broad swell and under the black frown of a wall of darker darkness against the jewelled southern sky.

The landing is a small concrete breakwater, into the crooked arm of which we slipped, trusting in the lantern gleam to dark hands of natives that reached to help. We wondered, entirely without alarm, if they were leprous fingers we grasped, but rested upon fate and climbed our best.

The wall was rimmed with sitting figures, and when our twenty-five leper passengers set foot on the cement, some were greeted in soft, hesitant Hawaiian speech as if by acquaintances. In the flicker of the swinging lanterns we glimpsed a white woman's anxious face and two pale hands stretched out. And tears were in my eyes to see the German mother and child united, even in their awful plight.

A quiet Japanese man took charge of me and my suit-case, and I was taken in a cart up a gentle rise to this cottage smothered in garden trees, the door of which I reached by way of a sweet-scented, viney walk. The night was almost grue-somely still, and I tried to pierce the gloom to judge how near was that oppressive wall to the south, but could form no idea in the velvet black. It was only darker than the rest of the darkness.

The Japanese turned me over to his wife, a tiny motherly thing who fluttered me into a bright white room with canopied bed, into which she indicated I was to plump forthwith ; that the bath was just across the lanai ; breakfast at eight ; and could she do anything for me ?

In a few moments Jack arrived, and we slept well into the new day. After breakfast the official " clean " members of the colony dropped in, Doctors Goodhue and Hollmann, the pioneer resident surgeon and his assistant, with their wives, as well as the German-Hawaiian parents of Mrs. Goodhue, who had tramped down the pali the previous day from their ranch in the highlands " beyond the pale," to visit their daughter. And Jack and I promptly registered the thought that if they could negotiate that trail, why not we ?

Never have we spent such a day of strange interest. Before luncheon, Mr. McVeigh drove us to within two or three hundred yards of the foot of the pali, to see the Kalaupapa Rifle Club at practice. And would you believe ? Quite as a matter of course we sat on benches side by side with the lepers, and when our turns came stood in their shooting boxes, and with rifles warm from their hands hit the target at 200 yards. Oh, I did not quite make the bull's-eye, but there were certain drawbacks to my best marksmanship—the heavy and unfamiliar gun that I had not the strength to hold perfectly steady, and the audience of curious men whose personal characteristics were far from quieting to malahini wahine nerves. Both of us were duly decorated with the proud red badge of the Club, bearing " Kalaupapa Rifle Club, 1907," in gilt letters.

But fancy watching these blasted remnants of humanity, lost in the delight of scoring, their knotted hands holding the guns, on the triggers the stumps of what had once been fingers, while their poor ruined eyes strove to run along the sights. . . .

It took all our steel, at first, to avoid shrinking from their hideousness ; but, assured as we were of the safety of mingling, our concern was earnestly to let them know we were unafraid of them. And it made such a touching difference. Out of their watchful silence and bashful loneliness they emerged into their natural care-free Hawaiian spirits.

For, you must know, all leprosy is not painful. There is what is termed the anæsthetic variety, which twists and deforms but which ceases from twinging as the disease progresses or is arrested, and the nerves go to sleep. Another and inexpressibly loathsome form manifests itself in running sores ; but Dr. Goodhue now takes prompt action on such cases, his brave, deft surgery producing marvellous results. Tubercular leprosy makes swift inroads and quick disposal of the sufferer. But it should make the public happier to know that here the majority of the patients come and go about the business of their lives as in other villages the world over, if with less beauty of face and form.

In the afternoon, Mr. McVeigh being much occupied after his vacation, Dr. Hollmann took us in charge, and showed us first the Bishop (Catholic) Home for Girls, presided over by Mother Marianne, the plucky aged Mother Superior of Hawaii Nei. Here she spends most of her life, two sisters living with her. Like a tall spirit she guided us across the playground and through schoolrooms and dormitories. In one of the latter we recognized a young girl who came on the *Noeau* last night. Standing in a corner talking with two friends whose faces were fairly obliterated, this latest comer neither looked nor acted as if there was anything unusual about them. She has a rare sense of adjustment, that girl—or else is mercifully wanting in imagination.

It seems that women are more susceptible to the ruin of disease, mental or physical, than their brothers—at least they show it more ruinously. I have noticed, in feeble-minded and insanity institutions that the eclipse of personality is more complete among the females. Perhaps it seems this way because we are used to especial comeliness in women, and to see a vacant or disfigured countenance above feminine habiliments instead of the sweet flower of woman's face, is dreadful beyond the dreadfulness of man's features under similar misfortune.

"Would you like to hear the girls sing?"

Like was hardly the word; I would have fled weeping from what could only be an ordeal to every one.   But we could not refuse good Mother Marianne the opportunity to display the talents of her pupils, and a Sister was dispatched to summon them.

Draggingly enough they came, unsmilingly, their bloated or contracted features emerging grotesquely from the clean holokus.   Every gesture and averted head showed a piteous shame over lost fairness—a sensitive pridefulness that does not seem to trouble the male patients.

Clustered round a piano, one played with hands that were not hands—for where were the fingers? But play she did, and weep I did, in a corner, in sheer uncontrol of heartache at the girlish voices gone shrill and sexless and tinny like the old French piano, and the writhen mouths that tried to frame sweet words learned in happier days. They looked dumbly at the white wahine who grieved for them—indeed, for some moments it would have been difficult to say who was sorrier for the other.   Out of their horrible eyes they watched us go, and I wonder if Jack's sad face and my wet cheek were any solace to them.   But they called " Aloha " bravely as we went down the steps, as did a group of girls under a hau tree—one of whom, a beautiful thing, crossing the enclosure with the high-breasted, processional carriage of the Hawaiian, showed no mark of the curse upon her swart skin where the young blood surged in response to our greeting.

The Bay View Home was our next objective, in which live the most advanced cases of the men. Nothing would do but Jack would see everything to be seen—and where he goes and can take me, there does he wish me to go to learn the face, fair and foul, of the world in which we live. And here we came across several of our own race, with whom we talked, and they appeared quite cheerful—let us say philosophical. One in particular, a ghastly white old man whose eyes hung impossibly upon his cheeks, spoke with the gentlest Christian fortitude, trying to smile with a lip that fanned his chest—I do not exaggerate. Only one there was who seemed not in the slightest resigned—he who led us among his brother sufferers in this house of tardy dissolution.

"Do any of them ever become used to their condition?"

His terrible eyes came down to my face with a look of utter hopelessness.

"I have been here twenty-five years, Mrs. London, and I am not used to it yet."

Glancing back from the gate, we saw him still standing on the lanai, straight and tall, gazing out over the sea; a man once wealthy and

honoured in his world—a senator, in fact. And
now there remains nothing before him after his
twenty-five disintegrating years of exile, but long
years of the same to follow, at the end of which
he sees himself, an unsightly object, laid in the
ground out of the light of heaven.

There is one hope, always, for those of the
lepers who think—the shining hope that blessed
science, now aroused, may discover at any
illuminated moment the natural enemy of the
bacillus leprae which has been isolated and become
thoroughly familiar to the germ specialists.
Jack, visiting the Kalihi Detention Home and
Experiment Station, in Honolulu, in company
with Mr. Pinkham, was shown the *bacillus leprae*
under the microscope. Plans are under way for
a federal experiment laboratory and hospital on
Molokai for the study of the evil germ. "The
dirty beast ! " Jack mutters under his breath.
The Settlement itself is a territorial care, managed
by the Board of Health.

In another building we inspected the little
dispensary, and here met Annie Kekoa, a half-
white telephone operator from Hilo, on Hawaii,
daughter of a native minister. One of her small
hands is very slightly twisted ; otherwise she is
without blemish, and very charming—educated
and refined, with the loveliest brown eyes and
heart-shaped face. Being a deft typewriter, she is
employed in the dispensary to fill her days, for
she is entirely unreconciled to her changed condition. Little she spoke of herself, but was eager

for news of Honolulu and our own travels. We
told her of a resemblance she bears to a friend
at home, and she said in a shaken voice : " When
you see your friend again, tell her she has a little
sister on Molokai." At the moment of parting,
a sudden impulse caused us both to forget the
rules, and we reached for each other's hands.
I know I shall never be sorry.

" Major " Lee, one-time American engineer in
the Interisland Steamship Company, demon-
strated the workings of a newly installed steam
poi-factory. He was in the gayest of humours,
and ever so proud of his spick-and-span machinery.
" We're not so badly off here as the Outside
chooses to think," he announced contentedly,
patting a rotund boiler. And then, with explosive
earnestness : " I say, Mr. London give 'em a
breeze about us, will you ? Tell 'em how we
really live. Nobody knows—nobody has told
half the truth about Molokai and the splendid
way things are run. Why, they give the impression that you can go around with a basket and
pick up fingers and toes and hands and feet.
They don't take the trouble to find out the truth,
and nobody seems to put 'em straight. Why,
leprosy doesn't work that way, anyhow. Things
don't *fall off* : they *take up*—they absorb. We've
got our pride, you know, and we don't like the
wrong thing believed on the Outside, naturally.
So you give the public a breeze about us, Mr.
London, and you'll have the gratitude of the
fellows on Molokai."

And I thought I saw, in Jack's active eye, a hint of the fair breeze to a gale that he would set ablowing on the subject of " the fellows on Molokai."

When " Major " Lee sailed his last trip on the old Line, the luckier engineers of the *Noeau*, taking him to Kalaupapa, said : " Come on down to our rooms, and be comfortable." Lee protested—No, it would not be right ; it wouldn't be playing the game ; he was a leper now, a leper, do you hear ?   and things were different, old fellows. . . .   " Different, your granny ! " and with friendly oaths and suspicious movements of shirt sleeves across eyes, the chief and his men had their old comrade into their quarters and gave him the best they had, even to a stirrup-cup—an infringement of orders, as alcohol is the best accomplice of leprosy.

Leaving Kalaupapa, we drove across the peninsula to the elder village, Kalawao, where the sainted Damien came to bury himself alive in days when conditions were vastly different from those of the sane and sanitary system now prevailing.

. The villages are a bare mile apart by Damien Road, and midway Dr. Hollmann turned to the left up a short steep rise, from the top of which our eyes dropped into a tiny crater—deep, emerald cup jewelled with red stones, a deeper emerald pool in the bottom, fringed with clashing sisal swords.   We came near having a more intimate view of the inverted cone, for a sudden powerful gust of the strong trade that sweeps the peninsula caught us off guard and obliged us to lean sharply back against the blast. Descending the outer slopes of the miniature extinct volcano, we poked around for a while amidst some nameless graves, the old cement mounds and decorations crumbling to dust. The place was provocative of much speculation upon human destiny.

In Kalawao we called at the Catholic Home for Boys, presided over by Father Emmerau and the brothers, and met up with Brother Dutton, veteran of the Civil War, Thirteenth Wisconsin, who later entered the priesthood, and has immolated himself for years among the leper youth. We found him very interesting, as he found Jack, with whose career he proved himself well acquainted.

And then across the road to a little churchyard, we stood beside the tombstone of Father Damien —name revered by every one who knows how this simple Belgian priest came to no sanitary, law-abiding, well-ordered community such as to-day adorns the shunned triangle of lowland. He realized his destination before he leaped from the boat ; and, once ashore, did not shrink nor turn back from the fearful duty he had imposed upon himself. A life of toil and a horrible lingering death were the forfeit of this true martyr of modern times. We have seen photographs of him in the progressing stages of his torment, and nothing more frightful can be conjured.

Never did we think to stand beside his grave. Just a little oblong plot of carefully tended green, enclosed in iron railing, with a white marble cross and a foot-stone—that is all ; appropriately simple for the simple worker, as is the Damien Chapel alongside, into which we stepped with the Bishop, our fellow-passenger on the *Noeau*, and Fathers Emmerau and Maxime, to see the modest altar. Standing there before the plain shrine in the subdued light, it seemed as if there could have been no death for the devoted young foreign priest who came so far to lay down his life for his friends.

After a delicious dinner cooked by the pretty Japanese Masa and her husband, during which I learned to like the sweet dried squid, the other household came over to our lanai. And while we talked, in through the twilight stole vibrations of swept strings, and the sob of a violin, and voices of the " Glee Club " of male singers that wove in perfect harmonies—voices thrilling as the metal strings but sharpened and thinned by the corroded throats of the singers. Think—think—there we sat in plenitude of health and circumstance, while at the gate, through which none but the clean may ever stray, outside the pale of ordinary human association, these poor pariahs, these shapes that once were men in a world of men, sang to us, the whole, the fortunate, who possess return passage for that free world, the Outside—lost world to them.

They sang on and on, the melting Hawaiian

songs, charming " Ua Like No a Like," and
" Dargie Hula," " Mauna Kea " beloved of Jack,
and his more than favourite, Kalakaua's " Sweet
Lei Lehua," with tripping, ripping hula airs unnumbered. At the end of an hour bewitched, to
Mr. McVeigh's low " Good night, boys," their
last Queen's own " Aloha Oe," with its fadeless
" Love to you," that has helped to make Hawaii
the Heart-Home of countless lovers the world
over, laid the uttermost touch of eloquence upon
the strange occasion. The sweet-souled musicians
who in their extremity could offer pleasure of
sound if not of sight to us happy ones, faded
away in the blue starlight, the hula-ing of their
voices that could not cease abruptly, drifting
faint and fainter on the wind.

KALAUPAPA,
Wednesday, July 3, 1907.

" Quick ! First thought ! *Where are you ? "*
Jack quizzed, as through the jasmine we peered
at a score of vociferous lepers running impromptu
horse-races on the rounding face of the green.
Remote, fearsome Molokai, where the wretched
victims of an Asiatic blight try out their own fine
animals for the prize events of the Glorious
Fourth ! " Some paradox," murmurs Jack. And
all forenoon we listen to no less than four separate
and distinct brass bands practising in regardless
fervour for the great day. Laughing, chattering
wahines bustled about the sunny landscape,

carrying rolls of calico and bunting; for they, too, will turn out in force on the morrow to show how the women of Hawaii once rode everywhere in the kingdom—following upon that gift of the first horse by Captain Cook to Kamehameha— astride in long flowing skirts of bright colours— the *pa'u* riders of familiar illustrations.

Mr. McVeigh, satisfaction limned upon his Gaelic countenance at all this gay preparation, is much occupied, together with his *kokuas* (helpers), in an effort to forestall another kind of conviviality that is unendingly sought by the lepers on their feast-days; and, denied all forms of alcohol, they slyly distil "swipes" from anything and everything that will ferment—even potatoes.

But the lusty Superintendent was not too busy to plan our entertainment for the afternoon, which took the shape of a ride to the little valleys of the pali. There was an odd assortment of mounts—every one of which, despite the appearance of two I could name, was excellent in its way. Mr. McVeigh's solid weight was borne by a big dapple-grey, while Dr. Hollmann bestrode a stocky bay; and Miss Kalama Myers, the strapping handsome sister of Mrs. Goodhue, sat a tall black charger. Jack's allotment was a stout, small-footed beastie, little larger than a Shetland, and to me fell a disappointingly tiny, gentle-seeming white palfrey. To my observant eye, Jack *looked* more than courtesy would allow him to express, for his appearance was highly ridiculous. Although of medium height, five feet nine inches, his feet hung absurdly near the ground, and his small Australian saddle nearly covered the pony's back.

We ambled along for a short distance, when our host's huge grey suddenly bolted, followed by the others, and I as suddenly became aware that my husband was no longer by my side. The next instant I was in the thick of a small stampede across country, the gentleness of the milk-white palfrey a patent delusion and snare, and Jack's inadequate scrap, leaping like a jack-rabbit, had outdistanced the larger horses. Every one was laughing uproariously, and Jack, now enjoying the practical joke played on us both, waved an arm and disappeared down Damien Road in a cloud of red dust.

Pulling up to a decorous gait through Kalawao, we left the peninsula and held on around the base of the pali till the spent breakers washed our trail, where a tremendous wall of volcanic rock rose abruptly on the right. The trail for the most part was over boulders covered with seaweed, and we two came to appreciate these pig-headed little horses whose faultless hoofs, unshod, carried us unslipping on the precarious footing.

Skirting the outleaning black wall, we looked ahead to a coast-line of lordly promontories that rise beachless from the peacock-blue deep water, between which are grand valleys inaccessible except by boat and then only in calm weather. Two of these valleys, Pelekunu and Wailau, contain settlements of non-leprous Hawaiians who live much as they did before the discovery of the islands, although they now sell their produce to the Leper Settlement.

Turning into the broad entrance of a quickly-narrowing cleft called Waikolu, we rode as far as the horses could go, and some pretty problems were set them on the sliding rocky trail. Then tethering them in the kukui shade, we proceeded on foot up a steep muddy path, where the vegetation, drenched overnight with rain, in turn drenched us and cooled our perspiring skins. Except for the trail—and for all we knew that might have been a wild pig run—the valley appeared innocent of man; but presently we gained to where orderly patches of water-taro, with its heart-shaped leaves, terraced the steep, like a nursery of lilies, and glimpsed idyllic pictures of grass-houses built on ferny ledges of the mountain-side, shaded by large-leaved banana and breadfruit trees, and learned that in these upland vales live certain of the lepers who, preferring an agricultural life, furnish the Settlement with vegetables and fruit.

Jack's imagination went aroving over the possibilities: " Why, look here, Mate Woman," he planned, " we could, if ever we contracted leprosy, live here according to our means. I could go on writing and earning money, and we could have a mountain place, a town house down in the village, a bungalow anywhere on the sea-shore that suited us, set up our own dairy with imported Jerseys, and ride our own horses, as well as sail our own yacht—within the prescribed radius, of course—and let Dr. Goodhue experiment on our cure!—Isn't it all practical enough ? " this to the grinning " Jack " McVeigh, who was regarding him with unconcealed delight, and who assured us he wished us no harm, but for the pleasure of our company he could almost hope the plan might come to pass !

Hours Jack spends " cramming " on leprosy from every book on the subject that the doctors have in their libraries. And literally it is one of the themes about which what is not known fills many volumes. The only point upon which all agree is that they are sure of nothing as regards the means by which the disease is communicated. The nearest they can hazard is that it is *feebly* contagious, and that a person to contract it must have a predisposition. Thus, one might enter the warm blankets of a leper just risen, and, by hours of contact with the effluvia therein, " catch " the disease. The same if one slept long in touch with a victim—and then only if one had the predisposition. And who is to know if the predisposition be his ? Certain theories as to the mode of contagion were given us as settled facts by the authorities of the Lazar Hospital in Havana, where we first became interested in leprosy ; but that there is little dependence to be placed on these opinions is borne out by at least two known cases on Molokai : one, a native who has remained " clean " though

G

living with a wife so far gone that she attends to her yearly babies with her feet ; and the other, a woman who has buried five successive leprous husbands, and has failed to contract the disease.

We recall that in Havana we were assured that no attendant, no white person living for years within the confines of the institution, had ever become afflicted ; and the same is held on Molokai —which reports make us, as visitors, feel secure. On the other hand, several of the few white men here assert that they are absolutely ignorant as to the means of their own contagion, not having, to their knowledge, been exposed. One of these is a village storekeeper, a healthy, hearty fellow whom we have seen riding about in smart togs on a good horse. He possesses but one spot—on one foot—which to date has neither increased nor diminished. When he discovered the " damned spot," promptly he reported himself to the Board of Health ; and here he makes the splendid plucky best of his situation.

No cure of leprosy has ever been discovered. But occasionally some patient is found upon bacteriological examination to have no leprosy in him—never having had leprosy. Such are discharged from the Settlement. And nine times out of ten, they do not want to go, and will practise any innocent fraud to retain residence in the place that has become a congenial home.

In some ways the inhabitants of this peninsula are the happiest in the world. Food and shelter are automatic ; pocket-money may be earned.

Several private individuals conduct stores.   The helpers, kokuas, are in the main lepers, and earn their salaries.   The Board of Health carries on agriculture, dairying, stock-raising, and the members of the colony are paid for their labour, and themselves own many heads of cattle and horses which run pasture-free.   The men own their fishing boats and launches, and sell fish to the Board of Health for Settlement use.   Sometimes a catch of 4000 lb. is made in a night.   It is not an unhappy community—quite the reverse. And their religions are not interfered with, which is amply shown by the six different churches that flourish here.   Also there is a Young Men's Christian Association.

Cautiously our Liliputian steeds crept or scrambled along crumbling trails ; and I overheard the Superintendent's undertone to Dr. Goodhue : " No malahini riders with us today ! " which is encouragement that we may be permitted to ride the coveted zigzag out of the Settlement.

Long we rested on the Goodhue lanai to-night, and long the shadowy leper orchestra serenaded beyond the hibiscus hedges, while some one recalled a story of Charles Warren Stoddard's *Joe of Lahaina*, in which a Hawaiian boy, bright companion of other days, crept to the gateway in the dusk, and there from the dust called to his old friend.   For ever separated, they talked of old times when they had walked arm in arm, and arms about shoulders, in sweet Lahaina.

KALAUPAPA,
Thursday, July 4, 1907.

This morning we were shocked from dreams by noises so strange as to make us wonder if we were not struggling in nightmare—unearthly cackling mirth, and guttural shoutings and half-animal cries that hurried us into kimonos and sandals to join our household at the gate where they were watching a scene as weird as the ghastly din.   Only a little after five o'clock, the atmosphere was fittingly vague, and overhead we heard the rasping cry of a bosun bird, *puae*.   In the eery whispering dawn there gambolled a score or so " horribles," men and women already horrible enough, God wot, and but thinly disguised in all manner of extravagant costumings.   They wore masks of home manufacture, in which the makers had unwittingly imitated the lamentable grotesquerie of the accustomed features of their companions—the lopping mouth, the knobby or almost effaced noses, flapping ears ;   while, equally correct in similitude, the colour of these false-true visages was invariably an unpleasant, pestilent yellow.   Great heaven !—do our normal countenances appear abnormal to them ?

Some of the actors in this serio-comic performance were astride cavorting horses, some on foot ;   and one, an agile clown in spots and frills, seemed neither afoot nor horseback, in a way of speaking, for he travelled in company with a trained donkey that lay down peaceably whenever it was mounted.   One motley harlequin, whose ghostly white mask did not conceal a huge bulbous ear, exhibited with dramatic gesture and native elocution a dancing bear personified by a man in a brown shag to represent fur.

And all the while the crowd kept up a running fire of jokes and mimicry that showed no mean originality and talent.

In the silvering light across the dewy hemisphere a cavalcade of *pa'u* riders took shape, coming on larger and larger with a soft thunder of thudding hoofs, wild draperies straight out behind in the speeding rush, and drawing up with a flourish, horses on haunches, before the Superintendent's house. The vivid hues of the long skirts began to grow in the increasing daylight— some of them scarlet, some blue, or orange, while one proud equestrienne sued for favour with a flaunting panoply of Fourth of July red, white, and blue.

Many of the girls were mercifully still comely, even pretty, and rode superbly, handling their curveting steeds with reckless grace and ease, and I could hear Jack's kodak, the same that he used in the Japanese Russian War three years ago, clicking repeatedly despite the early hour.

All forenoon these gala-coloured horsewomen trooped singing and calling over the rises and hollows of the country-side, to incessant blaring of the bands of both villages combined. The whole was a picture of old Hawaii not to be found elsewhere in the whole territory, and certainly nowhere else in the world. For no set reproduction of the bygone customs could equal this whole-souled exhibition, costumed from simple materials by older women who remembered days of the past, carried out in the natural order of life in one of the most beautiful spots in the islands, if not on the globe. No description can depict the sight that was ours the forenoon long. Jack was wordless so far as concerned his work, and gave up to the enjoyment of the experience.

To our distress, we were appointed, along with Mrs. Myers, to award prizes at the race-track. We feared " getting in wrong," as Jack put it, by injudicious choices among the contestants, with whom we wanted to leave a fair impression. But Jack McVeigh pooh-poohed our diffidence, and insisted that we serve on the committee. Horseback we went to the races, and found the track like any other, with its grand-stand, its judges, its betting and bickering—the betting running as high as $150.00—its well-bred horses, and wild excitement when the jockeys came under the wire.

Jack tied his fractious pony, and I saw him on foot over by the judges' stand, waving arms and cowboy hat and yelling himself hoarse, just as crazy as the crowd of lepers he jostled, who were as crazy as he. I knew he was having the time of his life, close to life as it is lived on Molokai oversea. Later, he was conversing soberly with a Norwegian and his wife, both patients, who told us we had no idea what it meant to them all for us to come here and mingle among them as friends, and that the people were very happy about it. This was sweet tidings, for the lepers are so little forward in manners that invariably we must accost them first, whereupon they break into the smiling " Aloha " of their land.

Between heats, there were foot-races, and screaming sack-races, races to the slowest, in which Jack McVeigh figured on the rump of a balking donkey, and won ; then followed a wahine contest of speed, and a wahine horse-race.

But the most imposing event of the afternoon, as of the morning, was enacted by the *pa'u* riders, who paced leisurely in stately procession once around the course, then circled once in a swinging canter, and, finally, with mad whoopings, broke into a headlong stampede that swept twice and a half around before the Amazons could win control of their excited animals.   A truly gorgeous spectacle it was, the flying horses with their streaming beribboned tails, the glowing riders, long curling hair outblown, and floating draperies painting the track with brilliant colour—all mortal decay a thing forgot of actors and onlookers alike, in one grand frolic of bounding vitality and youth.

" Can you beat it !   Can you beat it ! " Jack panted ecstatically.

The three prizes were for $5.00, $3.00, and $2.00, and it would not be guessing widely to say that they came out of the private pocket of Mc-Veigh, along with numerous other gifts during the

day. He is not the man to go about with his
heart's good intentions pinned on his sleeve—
indeed, a supersensitive character would be out
of place as manager of such an institution ; but
hand in hand with iron will and executive ability,
he carries a heart as big as the charge he keeps,
and a keen grey eye quick to the needs of his
children, as he calls them.

The three delighted winners galloped abreast
once around the track and then rode out ; but
suddenly the buxom wahine, bright and bold of
eye and irresistible of smile, who had taken
second, wheeled about and came to attention
before the judges' stand with the request, to our
great surprise, that I ride once around with her.
" Oh, do, do ! " Jack under his breath instantly
prompted me, fearing I might hesitate to make
myself so conspicuous. Of course I mounted
forthwith, and together we pranced the circuit,
to deafening cheers from hundreds of throats.

But I was not riding with a leper, as we had
thought, for it turned out that this inviting girl
is a kokua, an assistant at the surgery, from
whom the bid to ride with her was in the best
Kalaupapa social usage.

The Superintendent's big dinner was a signal
triumph. Mr. McVeigh handled his mixed company with rare tact, several factions being represented. But even the grave and gentle Bishop
Liebert and the Fathers warmed to his kindly
and ready humour, and soon all were under the
spell of Kalama's perfumed garlands and the

really sumptuous feast that Masa and her husband, aided by the ladies, had prepared.   Jack
and I were in still raptures over Mrs. Goodhue,
whose sparkling beauty, crowned with a scarlet
carnation lei, was something to gladden the heart.

Then Mr. McVeigh rose and raised his glass to
" The Londons—Jack and Charmian, God bless
them ! "   And went on to confess to a warm
regard that touched us deeply.   For he has
given us his confidence during the past day or
two in a way that has mightily pleased us.   At
the end of the little speech, breaking into his
engaging smile of eyes and lips, he announced
that he knew all present would wish us well upon
our departure, which was approaching all too
soon, etc., etc., and which would be via the pali
trail ; and that Mrs. London should ride the best
horse on Molokai—his mule Makaha !

When the orchestra had opened with " Star
Spangled Banner " and several Hawaiian selec-
tions, a willowy young woman, graceful as a
nymph but with face as horrible as her body was
lovely, rendered a popular lightsome song in
tones that had lost all semblance to music.   Half-
caste she is, travelled and cultured, once a beauty
in Honolulu, whose native mother's bank account
is in seven figures.   And this girl, in the blossom-
time of life, with death overtaking in long strides,
bereft of comeliness, awful to behold, and having
known the best that life has to bestow, rises
superior to life and death, and, foremost in
courage, surpasses the gayest of her sisters in

misfortune.   What material for a Victor Hugo !

Following the musical programme, we left the fantastic company dancing as lustily as it had sung and laughed and ridden the day through. No one, listening outside to the unrestrained merry-making, could have guessed the band of abbreviated human wrecks, their distorted shadows monstrous in the flickering lamplight, performing, unconcernedly for once, their Dance of Death.

.   KALAUPAPA,
Friday, July 5, 1907.

Let no one say that great men, capable of noble martyrdom, have ceased from the earth in this day and age.   And Dr. William J. G. Goodhue, with his exceeding modesty, would be the first to protest any association of his pleasant name with such holy company.   But no outsider, entering upon the scene of his wonderful and precarious operations in tissue and bone diseased with the mysterious curse of the ages, could doubt that he had come face to face with one who spares himself not from peril of worse than sudden death.

Ungloved, his sole protection vested in caution against abrading his skin, and an antiseptic washing before and after his work, the man of empirical science waded elbow-deep into the unclean menace upon the operating table.   He was assisted by two women nurses, one Hawaiian, one Portuguese, and both with a slight twist of anæsthetic leprosy.

The first subject to-day was a middle-aged wahine, jolly and rolling fat, who was borne in laughing, and borne out laughing again. In between were but a few self-pitying moans when she raised her head to watch the doctor. We had every proof that she knew no pain, nor even discomfort ; but the sight of copiously flowing blood caused her to weep and wail " Auwe ! " until one of the nurses said something that made her laugh in spite of herself. The sole of her foot had thickened two inches, and she had not stepped upon it for a couple of years. Into this dulled pad, lengthwise, the cool surgeon cut clean to the diseased bone, which he painstakingly scraped, explaining that the blood itself remains pure, only the tissues and bone being attacked by the *bacillus leprae*.

But the second patient, a good-looking lad who came on the *Noeau* with us, had a terrible case of the most loathsome and agonizing sort, which made it necessary to anæsthetize him— Dr. Hollmann using the slow and safe " A.C.E." (Alcohol, one part, Chloroform, two parts, Ether, three parts). The only visible spot was a running sore forward of and below the left shoulder ; but what appeared on the surface was nothing to that which the knife divulged !

Although the details are not pretty, and I shall not harrow with more of them, I wish I could picture the calm, pale surgeon, with his intensely dark.blue eyes and the profile of Ralph Waldo Emerson, whose kinsman he is, working with master-strokes that cleansed the fearful cavity of corruption ; for it was an illustration of the finest art and beauty of which the human is capable.

And now this boy may possibly be quite healthy for the rest of a natural life, and die of some other malady or of old age. Again, the bacillus at any time may resume its destructive inroads elsewhere in his system. There are myriad unknown quantities about leprosy. All Dr. Goodhue, with his sad and charming smile, can say about it with finality, is :—

" The more I study and learn about leprosy, the less assurance I have in saying that I know anything about it ! "

By this evening all troubadour spirit was quenched, and no minstrelsy greeted our post-prandial lolling on the lanai. No voice above a night-bird's disturbed the quiet of tired Kalaupapa. And we also were tired, for seeing the operations, although not our first, claimed a certain measure of nervous energy ; besides, we had ridden hard to another rugged valley in the late afternoon, goat-hunting on the crags, and were ready for early bed. In passing, I must not forget to relate that we were shown some black-and-white striped mosquitoes up-valley, the proper carriers of yellow fever—though heaven forbid that they ever have a chance to carry it !

Mr. and Mrs. Myers, those delightful souls, to-day ascended the baking pali on foot, to prepare for our coming on the morrow, when we shall have

accomplished the hair-raising way of the long
forbidden exit from Kalaupapa. Now that permission has been graciously accorded, the witty
Jack McVeigh enlarges continually upon the
difficulties and dangers of the route.

WAIKIKI,
Sunday, July 7, 1907.

At eleven o'clock yesterday, on our diminutive
animals, we bade forewell to our friends under the
cluster of kukuis where they had accompanied us
on the beginning of the ascent, and proceeded to
wage the sky-questing, arid pathway, for this
section of the pali is almost bare of. vegetation.
Short stretches as scary we have ridden ; it is
the length of this climb that tries—angling upon
the stark face of a 2300-foot barrier.

They told me, when I bestrode the strong back
of the little mule Makaha, to " stay by her until
the summit is reached. She never fails." Im-
plicitly I obeyed, for the very good reason that
I would have been loath to trust my own feet,
let alone my head. Never a stumble did the tiny
twinkling hoofs make, even where loose stony
soil crumbled and fell 1000 feet and more into
the sea that wrinkled oilily far below ; and the
hardy muscle and lungs of her seemed to put forth
no unusual effort. But Jack and the Hawaiian
mail-carrier who led the way, were obliged
several times to dismount where the insecure
vantage was too much for the quivering, dripping
ponies, although they are well accustomed to the

work. Once, from the repairing above, some
rubble fell, fortunately curving clear. Makaha,
who has a few rudimentary nerves of her own,
shied, but instantly recovered, only to shy again
at a bag of tools by the trailside.

Sometimes an angle was so acute that our
beasts were forced to swing on hind-legs to reach
the upper zigzag, where poised front hoofs must
grip into sliding stones or feel for hold amidst
large fixed rocks, and the rider lay himself on the
horse's neck. A miss meant something less than a
half-mile of catapultic descent through blue space
into the blue ocean. Again, Jack glimpsed
destruction from the guide's horse that slipped
and scrambled and almost went off the zigzag
immediately overhead. I, at a turn below, saw
the peril to Jack, and knew my first real anxiety.
But the grey pony regained his feet amid flying
gravel. There were places where it seemed
incredible that anything less agile than a goat
could stick ; but the proof of the pudding . . .
and we live to tell the tale.

" Gee ! I don't wonder McVeigh won't let
malihinis go out this way," Jack called down,
craning his neck to see the base of the sea-washed
rampart, and failing. " It is worse than its
reputation ! "

The Settlement lay dreaming in the noonday
sun, like the green map of a peninsula stretched
in a turquoise sea. And we amused ourselves,
while resting the animals, picking out landmarks
familiar to us.

" There's McVeigh's house, and the Doctor's, where you see that bunch of trees," Jack pointed, " and I'll bet he's following us every inch with that telescope of his. Let's wave our arms for luck."

A short distance from the summit we joined the rebuilt portion of the trail, and passed the time of day with the stolid Japanese labourers and their bright-eyed foreman. Six feet wide, some parts railed, to our pinched vision it appeared a spacious boulevard. Our sensations, now speedily at the top and looking over, must have been something like those of Jack of Beanstalk fame when he found a verdant level plain at the end of his clambering. Here was a prairie of green hillocks browsed by fat cattle, and threaded by a red road. A roomy family carriage waited, driven by a stalwart son of the Myers', and we parted from the guide, patting our little beasts before he led them back to the " falling-off-place." A mule of parts, that canny small Makaha. I shall not see her like again.

The restful drive of a couple of miles through rich pasture land dotted with guava shrub brought us to the home of the Myers family, in the midst of a 60,000-acre ranch. There are no hotel facilities whatever on Molokai, which is forty miles long by ten in breadth, and the visitor not lucky enough to have friends and friends of friends on the island, will see little unless he comes equipped for camping. The climate in these islands is mild and cool, the hills and ruggeder mountains interspersed with meadows, where spotted Japanese deer have become so numerous that shooting them is a favour to the ranchers. Kalama, that fine all-round sport, had begged us to come some time and go with her for a week's hunting.

High Molokai should be a paradise for sportsmen, and it is surprising the territory does not get together with the owners and try to develop facilities at Kaunakaki for housing, and transportation into the back country, which is surpassingly beautiful and interesting. Somewhere on the coast there is an old battle-field where countless human bones still whiten ; and on the rocky coast to the south can be seen in shallow water the ruins of miles of ancient fish-ponds equalled nowhere in the group. On the north-west one sees Oahu, cloud-capped and shimmering in the blue, while Haleakala bulks 10,000 feet in air on Maui to the east.

This ranch home is buried in flowers, and my unbelief in begonias a dozen feet high underwent rude check. A fairy forest of them surrounds the guest-cottage, casting a rosy shadow on window and lanai. I should have been content to remain here indefinitely. Little Miss Mabel, sweet sixteen, entertained us charmingly, and during luncheon, served by a butterfly maid of Japan, the telephone jingled, and Kalama down in Kalaupapa was telling us to be sure to swim in the cement irrigation reservoir before starting for the hot drive to the steamer. Which we did, and many thanks.

On the ten-mile rolling descent to the port, Kaunanakai, there was ample chance to observe this side of the supposedly melancholy isle, and Jack, noticing dry creeks and the general thirsty appearance of the lower foothills, descanted upon its rich future when some irrigation schemes are worked out and applied. As it is now, only in the rainy season do the streams flow.

Dashing native cowboys, bound for a wedding luau, passed us on the road, teeth and eyes flashing, gay neckerchiefs about their singing brown throats, and hat-brims blown back from their vivid faces, out-Westing the West.

Kaunanakai itself is not especially attractive, and during two hours' waiting for the Iwilani, we occupied ourselves keeping as comfortable as possible, for July is hot on the leeward sides of the " Sandwich Islands."

Once aboard, and our luggage, taken on at Kalaupapa, safely located, we watched the loading of freight and live stock on the little steamer. Between the deep rolling of the ship and the din and odour of seasick swine for'ard, there was little rest the night. And the Steamship Company has a very unceremonious way of dumping its passengers ashore in Honolulu at the most heathenish hours. The car-lines had not yet started when we stood yawning and chill beside our bags and saddles on the wharf, and Jack was obliged to wake a hackman to drive us to Waikiki. The city lay dead but for an occasional milk-waggon, and after all we did not grudge ourselves

the dawning loveliness of the morning over duck-
ponds and reef, valley and mountain, and Diamond Head seemed like an old friend. Tochigi
had to be roused at the brown tent, and despite
drowsiness Jack plunged into an accumulation
of mail and other work before breakfast.

And all through the busy morning hours, and
the surf-boarding and swimming and romping
of the afternoon, of all the remarkable impressions
of that astounding week on Molokai, the pali
endured. Again and again we seemed to cling
to the impossible face of it, creeping foot by foot,
alert, tense, unafraid except for each other. . . .[1]

Wᴀɪᴋɪᴋɪ,
Thursday, July 11, 1907.

In a fine frenzy to give a just presentation of
the Leper Settlement, Jack has lost no time
finishing the promised article, " The Lepers of
Molokai," landing into the fascinating theme in
this wise :—

" When the Snark sailed along the windward
coast of Molokai, on her way to Honolulu, I
looked at the chart, then pointed to a low-lying
peninsula backed by a tremendous cliff varying
from two to four thousand feet in height, and
said : ' The pit of hell, the most cursed place
on earth.' I should have been shocked if, at that
moment, I could have caught a vision of myself a
month later, ashore in the most cursed place on

[1] A few weeks after our ascent, one of the Japanese
labourers fell 1,500 feet in the clear.

earth, and having a disgracefully good time along with 300 of the lepers who were likewise having a good time. Their good time was not disgraceful ; but mine was, for in the midst of so much misery it was not meet for me to have a good time. That is the way I felt about it, and my only excuse is that I could not help having a good time.''

He goes on with a picture of himself yelling at the trackside with the lepers when the horses came under the wire, and presently branches off into a serious consideration of the situation, interspersed with bright items of life in the Settlement. The article is highly approved by Mr. Pinkham, and Mr. Thurston avers it is the best and fairest that has ever been written. Jack is modestly elated, because he has succeeded in pleasing both these men who are far from friendly in the general affairs of the territory. And, best of all to Jack, in all honest enthusiasm he has pleased himself.

Although the President of the Board of Health is entirely satisfied with himself and with the article, as well as with Jack's press interviews regarding the trip, several prominent citizens have expressed themselves to the official as highly indignant that we should have been allowed in the Settlement. But the imperturbable Pinkham has told them with asperity that it does not profit them or Hawaii to imitate ostriches and simulate obliviousness of the fact that the world knows of leprosy in Hawaii. And why should Hawaii be supersensitive ! Leprosy is not unknown in the large cities even of America ; and Hawaii should be proud to advertise her magnificent system of segregation, unequalled anywhere in the world, and be glad to have it exploited by men of conscience and intelligence.

WAILUKU, MAUI,
Sunday, July 24, 1907.

Two evenings gone, in company with Mr. and Mrs. Thurston, we boarded the *Claudine*, which, though much larger than the *Noeau*, pitched disgustingly in the head-sea of Kaiwi Channel, and took more than spray over the upper deck for'ard where were our state-rooms. Jack and I fell unexpectedly sick, and our friends likewise, although not unexpectedly. Lorrin Thurston has traversed these channels since boyhood, and never does he cease from acute suffering during frequent crossings.

A swarm of Japanese sailed steerage and outside on the lower deck, each bearing a matted bundle exactly like his neighbour's, the women carrying their possessions wrapped in gorgeously coloured challies in which a stunning orange was most conspicuous among vivid blues and greens and intermediate purples. Early in the trip all were laid low in everything but clamour, and from our deck we could see the poor things in disheartened deshabille, pretty matron and maiden alike careless of elaborate chignon falling awry, the men quite chivalrously trying to ease their women's misery in the pauses of their own.

Kahului, our destination, is on the northern shore of the isthmus connecting West Maui with the greater Haleakala section of the practically double island ; but Mr. Thurston's emotions were of such intensity that around midnight he staggered weakly to our latticed door and suggested we disembark at Lahaina, the first port, finish the night at the hotel, and in the morning drive around the peninsula of West Maui to Wailuku.

Nothing loath to escape the roughest part of the passage, doubling that disturbing headland, we dressed and gathered our hand-luggage ; and at half-past one in the morning dropped over the *Claudine's* swaying black side.   As we clung in the chubby, chopping boat, manned by natives with long oars, dimly we could make out dark towering heights against the starry sky, and on either side heard the near breakers swish and hiss warningly upon the coral.   And all about, near and far, burned the slanting flares of fishermen, the flames touching the black water with elongated dancing sparkles.   Voices floated after from the anchored steamer, and ghostly hoof-beats clattered faint but clear from the invisible streets of the old, old town.   As at Molokai, shadowy hands helped   us   upon   the   wharf—and   the   soft witchery of the night fled before the babble of hackmen, stamping of mosquito-bitten horses, a lost and yelping dachshund pup that insisted on being trod upon, and the huge red-faced hotel proprietor of an unornamental wooden hostelry, the dingy entrance lighted with smoking kerosene lamps.

"Beautiful Lahaina," warbled Isabella Bird Bishop, in her charming book *Hawaii* : "Sleepy Lahaina," she ecstatically trills—and she is not the only writer who has sung the praises of this town of royal preference, once the prosperous capital of the kingdom, and the oldest white settlement, where touched the whaling ships that sometimes anchored fifty strong off shore. But this prosperity entailed disease and death, since the adventurous sailors were given free run by their unscrupulous captains. The village dwindled to less than a wraith of its former opulence, much of the original site now being planted to cane. A little distance above, the old Lahainalua Seminary, founded in 1831, still flourishes, maintaining its reputation as an excellent industrial school. At the start the scholars supported themselves by cultivating land granted by the chiefs to the school, and were obliged to build the schoolhouse and their own lodgings. Later on a printing-press and book-bindery were established, and the institution did much of the printing of text-books in use. The very first Hawaiian sheet, *Lama Hawaii*, was published here, preceding the *Kumu Hawaii*, at Honolulu.

And the reader of Isabella Bird yearns for Lahaina above all bournes ; he cannot wait to test for himself Lahaina's spell of loveliness and repose. But this repose must belong to the broad day, or else the gallant lady's mosquito-net was longer than ours, which cruelly refused to make connection with the coverlet. Jack's priceless perorations will ever be lost to posterity, for I shall repeat them not.

In the morning, Mrs. Thurston peeped laughingly in and asked if I knew my husband's whereabouts ; and I, waking alone, confessed that I did not, although I seemed to recall his desertion in a blue cloud of vituperation against all red-headed hotel hosts and stinging pests. Mrs. Thurston, viewing the blushing morn from the second-story veranda, had come upon the weary boy fast asleep on the hard boards, blanket-over-head, and led me to where he lay. But none more vigorously famished than he, when we sat in an open-air breakfast-room, table spread with land-fruit and sea-fruit ; for Mr. Thurston had been abroad early to make sure the meal should be an ideal one after our hard night —fish from the torchlight anglers, alligator pears dead-ripe out of the garden, and the famous luscious mangoes of Lahaina, the best in the islands.

" And me for the good coffee ! " Jack appreciated, for he suspicioned that the quiet but efficient man had been also in the kitchen, and he loves his coffee when it *is* coffee. Rather reticent upon first acquaintance, Mr. and Mrs. Thurston have blossomed into the most cordial and witty of comrades, ready for anything.

Mrs. Bishop, in the '70's, spoke of Lahaina

as " an oasis in a dazzling desert." [1]   The dazzling desert has been made to produce the cane for two great sugar mills whose plantations spread their green over everything in sight to the feet of the sudden mountains rent by terrific chasms rising 6000 feet behind the village.   Once this was a missionary centre as well as the regular port of call for the devastating whale ships.   The deserted missionary house, fallen into decay these long years, is still a landmark of a Lahaina that but few live to remember.

The streets of the drowsy town are thickly shaded by coconuts, breadfruit with its glossy truncated leaves and green globes, monkey-pod kukui, bananas, and avocadoes ; and before we bade farewell to Lahaina, Mr. Thurston drew up beside an enormous mango tree, benefactor of his boyhood, where the obliging Hawaiian policeman, in whose garden it grows, with his pretty wife threw rocks to bring down a lapful of the ripe fruit—deep-yellow, with rosy cheeks, a variety known as the " chutney " mango.

It is some twenty-three miles from Lahaina to Wailuku, and the road runs for a distance through tall sugar-cane, then begins an easy ascent to where it is cut into the sides of steep and barren volcanic hills above the sea.   There was a glorious surf running, and for miles we could gaze almost straight down to the water, in some places catching glimpses of shoals of black fish in the blue brine

[1] Six Months in the Sandwich Islands, published by John Murray, London.

where there was no beach and deep ocean washed the feet of the cliffs.

Jack has blue-pencilled my description of the capital luncheon arranged in advance by Mr. Thurston, holding that although I write best on the subject of food, my readers may become bored. So I shall pass on to Iao Valley (E-ah-o —quickly E-ow) where we drove in the afternoon, following the Wailuku River several miles to the valley mouth.

Iao has been pronounced by travellers quite as wonderful in its way as Yosemite. I should not think of comparing the two, because of their wide difference. The walls of Iao are as high, but appear higher, since the floor, if floor it can be called, is much narrower. Most gulches in Hawaii draw together from a wide entrance ; but in Iao this is reversed, for, once the narrow ascending ingress is passed, the straight walls open like the covers of a book which Doré might have illustrated, the valley widening into an amphitheatre of unsurpassable grandeur. On the ferned and mossed walls of the entrance hung festoons of deep-trumpeted blue convolvulæ between slender dracenza palms and far-reaching branches of silvery kukuis, quivering or softly swaying in passing airs.

It is ridiculous to try to give any impression of the prodigious palisades, with their springing bastions, the needled peaks, the shimmering tropical growth of tree and vine, the bursting, sounding falls of water-courses rushing headlong

over mighty boulders, the swift-rolling glory of
clouds, casting showers of gold upon joyous
green pinnacles or with deep violet shadow turning these into awful fingers pointing to the zenith ;
nor can one fitly describe the climate—the
zephyrs warm and the wind-puffs cool that
poured over us where we lay on a table-land,
reached by a trail through a sylvan jungle of
ferns, in matted grass so deep and dense that we
never felt the solid earth.

Long we rested, surrounded by impregnable
fastnesses, speaking little, in an ecstasy of wonder-
ment at this superlatively grand and beautiful
cleft ; at its head, lord of all lesser peaks and
spires and domes, Puu Kukui springing 5780 feet
into the torn sky. There are other valleys back
of Puu Kukui, as beautiful as Iao, but more
difficult of access. It is said by the few who have
ascended that the view from the top of Puu
Kukui is away and beyond anything they have
ever seen.

There is but one way out of Iao, as usual in
these monster gulches of Hawaii, and that is the
way in. Old warriors learned this to their rue,
caught by Kamehameha in the sanguinary
battle that completed his conquest of Maui,
when their blood stained the water of the stream
as it flowed seaward, which henceforth bore the
name of Wailuku, " Red Water."

From our high vantage, looking seaward, down
past the interlacing bases of the emerald steeps
eroded by falling waters of æons, we beheld the

plains country beneath, all rose and yellow and green with cultivated abundance, bordered at the sea-rim by white lines of surf inside bays and out around jutting points and promontories, the sapphire deep beyond, and upon the utmost indigo horizon pillowy trade-clouds low-lying—all the splendour softened into tremulous, glowing mystic fairyland. " Hawaii herself, in all the buxom beauty, roving industry . . . with all the bravery and grace of her natural scenery."

One pursues one's being in Hawaii within an incessant atmosphere of wonder and expectation—ah, I have seen Yosemite, and the Alps, and the Swiss lakes ; but Hawaii is different, partaking of these, and still different, and more elusively wonderful. Even now, as I write of what our eyes have gloried in, they behold the mighty roofless Haleakala, ancient House of the Sun, its rugged battlements piercing two miles into the ether, above the cloud-banners of sunset.

HALEAKALA RANCH, MAUI,
Monday, July 15, 1907.

Believe—except one be deaf, dumb, and blind, there is no boredom in these islands. Indeed, one must avoid bewilderment among the myriad attractions that fill the days to overflowing. Little opportunity was ours to become acquainted with the old town of Wailuku, with its picturesque population of natives and immigrants, for yesterday's programme included a private-car trip over the Hawaii Commercial and Kihei Sugar Companies' vast plantations. We were the guests of Mr. J. N. S. Williams, Superintendent of the Kahului Railroad Company, who met us at Kahului where we went aboard the car. There was a bustling air of activity and newness about the port town —track-laying, boat-loading, house-building ; and in the harbour, swung at anchor, a big freighter of the American-Hawaiian Line, unloading on lighters and receiving sugar by the same means.

Waving fields of cane occupy practically all the lowland between the two sections of Maui, spreading into the slopes of Haleakala's foothills and extending well around to the " Windward" side of the island. The trip included a visit to one of the mills and a descent some 400 feet into the shaft of Kihei's pumping station, where we were conducted by a young football giant from Chicago, Paul Bell, who was regretting that his work would prevent him from accepting an invitation to accompany our party through the crater.

At the village of Paia, with its streetful of alluring Japanese shops, we transferred to carriages for an eight-mile drive to this stock ranch 2000 feet up Haleakala. Seen from a distance, the mountain appears simple enough in conformation, smooth and gradual in rise. At closer range the rise is gradual, to be sure, but broken by ravines that are valleys, and by level pastures, ancient blow-holes and hillocks that are miniature mountains as perfect as Fujiyama. It is almost

disappointing —one has a right to expect more
spectacular perpendicularity of a 10,000-foot
mountain. Even now, from where we sit on
a shelf of lawn, under a tree with a play-house
in its boughs, it is impossible to realize that the
summit, free for once of cloud, is still 8000 feet
above, so lazily it leans back. And looking
downward, never have our eyes taken in so much
of the world from any single point.

Louis von Tempsky, English-Polish, son of the
last Bristish officer killed in the Maori War, handsome, wiry, military of bearing and discipline,
is manager of this ranch of 60,000 odd acres.
He came to Hawaii years ago on a vacation from
his New Zealand bank cashiership, and he never
went back—" shanghaied," says Jack. One cannot blame the man. Here he is able to live
to the full the life he loves, with those he loves
—the big free life of saddle and boundless miles,
with his own fireside (and one needs a fireside
up here of an evening) at the end of the day.
His wife, Amy, was born in Queen Emma's house
in Honolulu, of English parentage. Her father,
Major J. H. Wodehouse, was made English
Minister to Hawaii about three years before
annexation to the United States took place, and
now, back in England, is retired upon a pension.

And such a family they are—the beautiful
home-queen of a mother with the handsome
father of their sturdy brood, two daughters in
their early teens, who are boys in the saddle
and cowboys at that ; and a small maid of four,

Lorna, who rides her own pony. And lastly, a small precious son who is not quite old enough to cross a saddle-tree.

The climate is much like California's in the mountains, and very refreshing after the sea-level midsummer heat. This bracing air makes one feel younger by years. Life here would be ideal—a charming rambling old house, with a drawing-room that is half lanai, hung with good pictures, furnished with a good library and piano and fine-matted couches deep in cushions; a cosy dining-room where one comes dressed for dinner, and a commodious guest-wing where Jack and I have two rooms and bath, and he can work in comfort.

The lawn is a two-sided, sheltered court, intersected with red-brick walks, and lilies grow everywhere. From our books on the lawn beside a little fountain under tall trees where birds sing and twitter, we rise and step past the lilies to the edge of the garden, where the world falls away from our feet to the ocean. Standing as if in a green pavilion, we seem detached from the universe while viewing it. Terrace upon terrace of hills we see, champaigns of green speckled with little rosy craters like buds turned up to sun and shower; and off in the blue vault of sea and air, other islands, dim and palpitating like mirages. One hears that Maui, the second-largest island, contains 728 square miles and that it is 10,000 feet high; but what are figured confines when apparently the whole world of

land and sea is spread before one's eyes on every
hand ! Hand in hand we look, and look, and
try to grasp the far-flung magnitude of the vision,
feeling very small in the midst. " Beautiful's
no name for it," breathes Jack ; and through my
mind runs a verse of Mrs. Browning's, a favourite
of my childhood at Auntie's knee :—

We walk hand in hand in the pure golden ether
    And the lilies look large as the trees ;
    And as loud as the birds sing the bloom-loving bees—
And the birds sing like angels, so mystical-fine,
      While the cedars are brushing the Archangel's
        feet.
And Life is eternity, Love is divine,
    And the world is complete.

This morning early we were out looking at
our mounts and seeing that our saddles, brought
from home, were in good shape. " I love the
old gear ! " Jack said, caressing the leather,
well-worn on many a journey these two years.
For a cattle-drive and branding, with colt-
breaking to follow, were the business of the
day. At ten we galloped away from the corrals,
and Jack and I went right into the work with Mr
von Tempsky and his girls, Armine and Gwendolen,
and the native cowboys, to round up the cattle.
Oddly enough, although born and raised in the
West, we two have sailed over 2000 miles to experience our first *rodeo !*

To my secret chagrin, I was doomed to be
tried out upon an ambitionless mare, albeit
Louisa is well-gaited and good to the eye. But

I dislike to spur another person's animal, so took occasion to look very rueful when my host, coming alongside, inquired : " Are you having a good time ? " He could see that I was not, and sensed why ; so he advised me not to spare the spur, adding : " There isn't a better cattle pony, when she knows you mean business ! "

And oh, these " kanaka" horses with their sure feet ! And oh, the wild rushes across grassland that has no pitfalls—gophers are unknown here—thudding over the dustless, springing turf, hurdling the higher growth, whirling " on a cowskin " to cut off stray or wilful steers, and making headlong runs after the racing herd.   All the while, with Armine and Gwendolen, taking commands from General Daddy, and sitting tight our eager horses, fairly streaking the landscape in ordered flight to head off the runaways, the young girls with hair flying, sombreros down backs, cheeks glowing, eyes sparkling, utterly devoted to the work in hand—striving their best for ultimate praise from Daddy.

Miles we covered, doubling back and forth, searching out and driving the bellowing kine ; up and down steep ravines we chased them, along narrow soft-sliding trails on stiff inclines, turning to pathless footing to keep them going in the right direction.   And the farther afield we rode, the farther stretched the limitless reaches of that deceiving mountain.

At last the herds were converged toward a large gate not far from the outlying corrals, and

after a lively tussle we rounded up all but one
recalcitrant—a quarter-grown, black-and-white
calf that outran a dozen of us for half an hour
before we got him.

Promptly followed the segregation of those
to be marked ; the throwing of calves in the
dusty corral, and their wild blatting when the
cowboys trapped them, neck and thigh, with
the lasso ; the restless circling of the penned
beasts waiting their turns ; the trained horses
standing braced against lariats thrown from
their backs into the seething mass ; the rising,
pungent smoke of burning hair and hide as the
branding irons bit ; and the frantic scrambling
of the released ones to lose themselves in the
herd.

Together with several neighbours who had
ridden over, we sat fence-high on a little platform
overlooking the strenuous scene, and when the
branding was finished, the colt-breaking began
in which the von Tempsky children took the most
intense interest, as did we   Mr. von Tempsky
superintended his efficient force of native riders
in their work of handling three-year-old colts
that had never known human touch or feel of
rope, which made a Buffalo Bill show seem tame
indeed. For hours we sat almost breathless,
watching the making of docile saddlers, all being
subdued but one, which threatened to prove
an " outlaw." After the " buck " had been
taken out of the young things, they are tied up
all night to the corral fence, and in the morning

are expected to be tractable, with all tendency
to pull back knocked out of them for ever.

And some are sulky, while some will plunge,
    (*So ho ! Steady ! Stand still, you !*)
Some you must gentle, and some you must lunge,
    (*There ! There ! Who wants to kill you !*)
Some—there are losses in every trade—
Will break their hearts ere bitted and made;
Will fight like fiends as the rope cuts hard,
And die dumb-mad in the breaking-yard.

                      Ukulele, on Haleakala,
                        Tuesday, July 16, 1907.

Thirteen strong, we rode out from the ranch-
house this morning, on the second phase of our
week's trip in the crater and on around through
the Nahiku " Ditch " country.   Besides the cowboys, gladsome brown fellows all, overjoyed to
go along, there were seven in the party, with a
goodly string of pack-animals tailing out behind.
And bless my soul ! if there wasn't Louisa,
meekly plodding under a burden of tent-poles
and other gear.   For Mr. von Tempsky had now
allotted me his own Welchman, " the best horse
on the mountain," he declared.

5400 feet above sea level, our initial stop was
here at Ukelele, the dairy headquarters of the
ranch.   Why Ukulele, we are at loss to know,
for nothing about the place suggests that diminutive medium of harmony.   However, there is
a less romantic connotation, for the definition
of ukulele is literally " jumping flea."   But, as

Jack says, " Let us hope the place was called after the instrument ! "

The ascent we found steeper than below the ranch-house, but the climb worked no hardship on horse or rider. We were in good season to " rustle " supper and must go berrying for dessert. Of course, there had to be a berry fight between Jack and the two husky girls, who soon became weird and sanguinary objects, plastered from crown to heel with the large juicy *akalas* which resemble our loganberries. Jack asserts that they are larger than hens' eggs ; but lacking convenient eggs, there is no proving him in error. Nothing does him more good than a whole-hearted romp with young people, and Armine and Gwen were a match that commanded his wary respect. " I love to have my girls romp with Mr. London," once I heard a mother say. " He is like a clean-minded, wholesome boy, and never too rough."

After supper, we reclined upon a breezy point during a lingering sunset over the wide, receding earth, lifted high above the little affairs of men, and, still high above us, the equally receding summit. We felt light, inconsequential, as if we had no place, no weight, no reality—motes poised on a sliver of rock between two tremendous realities.

Mr. von Tempsky, resting his lithe, strong frame for once, recounted old legends concerning the House of the Sun, and the naming thereof, and the fierce warfare that is ever going on about its walls, between the legions of Ukiukiu and Naulu, the north-east trade and the leeward wind ; and until we were driven indoors by the chill, we lay about and watched the breezy struggle beneath among opposing masses of driven clouds.

And now, after a game of whist between Jack and Mrs. Thurston on the one side, and Messrs. Thurston and Von on the other, we are going to rest upon our *hikie* (hik-e-a), the same being a contrivance of hard boards, some seven feet square, covered with native mats and quilts made to measure.

PALIKU, CRATER OF HALEAKALA,
Wednesday, July 17, 1907.

And it's ho ! for the crater's rim, to look over ·to the mysterious Other Side from the tantalizing skyline that promises what no other horizon in all the world can give. Hail, Haleakala ! the largest extinct crater in existence ! It's boots and saddles for the unroofed House of the Sun. What will it be like ? (" Nothing you've ever seen or dreamed," this from the Thurstons). Shall we be disappointed ? (" Not if you're alive ! " contributes Mr. von Tempsky.) Jack gives me a heaving hand into the saddle, and a kiss by the way, and my Welchman strikes a swinging jog-trot that plays havoc with the opu-full—opu being stomach—with which my terrible mountain appetite has been assuaged.

Now the rolling grasslands give place to steep

and rugged mountain, with scant vegetation.
Here and there, relieving the monotony, is a
shining sheaf of silver blades, the " silver sword,"
with a red brand of blossoms thrusting from the
centre ; or patches of " silver verbena," a pretty
velvet flower that presses well and serves as
edelwiess for Haleakala. Stopping to breathe
the horses we nibble *ohelo* berries, which look
much like cranberries, but have a mealy-apple
flavour. There is wild country up here, where
sometimes cattle and ranging horses are pulled
down by wild dogs, and back in the fastnesses,
even mounted cowboys, rounding up the stock,
have been attacked.

And somebody is singing all the time. If
it is not Mr. Von's tenor, one hears Mr. Thurston's
pleasant voice on the breeze, essaying a certain
climacteric note that eludes his range at the
end of " Sweet Lei Lehua." A strong and
engaging character is Mr. Thurston, nervous,
alert under his firm-lipped smile ; a body quick
to steel into action ; hair greyed in service to
his islands ; keen black eyes shaded by thought-
ful brows, and eyes whose very colour frowns at
uncleanness or hypocrisy—eyes that reflect and
absorb humour at every turn. And there is
something imperious in his carriage and backward fling of head, that savours of courts and
kings and halls of statesmanship.

Over the sharp brittle lavas of antiquity our
horses, many of them barefooted, with hoofs
like onyx, scramble with never a fall on the pant-

ing steeps, on and on, up and up we forge with a blithe, lifting feel in the thin and thinner air, while the great arc of the horizon seems ever above the level of one's eye. And then comes a thrilling call from ahead that the next rise will land us on the jagged edge of the hollow mountain. I am about to join the charge of that last lap when a runaway packhorse—none other than Louisa, diverts my attention to the rear ; and when I turn again, the rest are at the top—all but Jack, who faces me upon his Pontius Pilate, until I come up. " Dear kid, I wanted to see it with you," he explains, and together we follow to Magnetic Peak—so-called what of its lodestone properties. And then . . .

More than twenty miles around its age-sculptured brim, the titanic rosy bowl lay beneath ; seven miles across the incredible hollow our gaze travelled to the glowing mountain-line that bounds the other side, and still above . . . we could not believe our sight that was unprepared for such ravishment of beauty. Surely we beheld very Heaven, the Isles of the Blest, floating above clouds of earth—azure snow-capped peaks so ineffably high, so ungraspably lovely, that we forgot we had come to see a place of ancient fire, and gazed spellbound from our puny altitude of 10,000 feet, upon illimitable heights of snow all unrelated to the burned-out thirsty world on which we stood.

It was only Mauna Kea—Mauna Kea and Mauna Loa, on the Big island of living fire,

half again as high as our wind-swept position ;
but so remote and illusive were they, that our
earthborn senses were incapable of realizing
that the sublime vision was anything more than
a daydream, and that we looked upon the same
lofty island, the highest on earth, that had greeted
our eyes from the *Snark*.

" It never palls," Armine whispered solemnly,
tears in her forget-me-not blue eyes. And her
father and Mr. Thurston, who had stood here
unnumbered times, soberly acquiesced. Jack
and I knew with certitude birthed of the magic
moment, that our memory, did we never repeat
our journeying, would remain undimmed for all
our days.

" But we are coming back some day ! " Jack
voiced his thought ; and then we devoted ourselves to hanging upon the glassy-brittle brink
and peering into the crater's unbelievable depths,
that are not sheer but slope with an immensity
of sweep that cannot be measured by the eye,
so deceptive are the red and black inclined
planes of volcanic sand.

Pointing to a small ruddy cone in the floor
of the crater, Mr. Thurston said ; " You would
hardly think that that blowhole is higher than
Diamond Head, but it is ! " And before there
was time to gasp and readjust our dazzled senses,
he was indicating an apparent few hundred feet
of incurving cinder-slope that looked ideal for
tobogganing, with the information that it was
over a mile in length. A dotted line of hoof-

prints of some wayward wild goat strung across
its red-velvet surface, and presently we were
tossing bits of lava over-edge upon unbroken
stretches immediately below, to watch the little
interrupted trails they traced until the wind
should erase them.   Only when the men loosened
large boulders into the yawning chasm, and we
saw them leaving diminishing puffs of yellow
ochre dust as they bounded upon the cinder-
sweeps, could we begin to line up the proportions
of the immediate crater-side, for whole minutes
were consumed, and minutes upon minutes, for
those swift stones to pass beyond sight.

" And why," queried Jack, " are we the only
ones enjoying this incomparable grandeur?
Why aren't there thousands of people climbing
over one another to hang all round the rim of
' the greatest extinct crater in the world ' ?   Such
a reputation ought to be irresistible.   Why there's
nothing on earth so wonderful as this !   I should
think there wouldn't be ships enough to carry
the tourists, if only for Iao and Haleakala.
Perhaps Hawaii doesn't want them, or need
them. . . .   Personally," he laughed, " I'm glad
my wife and I are the only tourists making a
racket here to-day.   And we're not tourists,
thank God ! "

Two broad portals there are into the House
Built by the Sun, and through them march the
warring winds, Ukiukiu and Naulu.   In at the
northern portal, Ukiukiu drives the trade-clouds,
mile-wide, like a long line of still, ghostly breakers,

only to have them torn to shreds, as to-day, and dissipated in the warm embrace of the rarefied airs of Naulu. Sometimes Ukiukiu meets with better luck, and fills the castle with cloud-legions ; but ours was the luck this day, for the crater was cleared of all but remnants of floating cloud-stuff, and our view was superb.

At last, tearing from the absorbing spectacle, we descended a short way to a stone-walled corral where the bright-eyed, sweet-mannered cowboys had lunch waiting—a real roughing-it picnic of jerked beef and salt pork, products of the ranch ; and hard-poi, called *pai'ai*, thick and sticky, royal pink-lavender poi, in a big sack. Into this we dug our willing fists, bringing them out daubed with the hearty substance. It came to me, blissfully licking the paíai from my fingers, that this promiscuous delving for poi into one receptacle that obtains among the natives, and which the real kamaaina is not afraid to emulate, is far from the unfastidious custom it is sure to appear upon first sight. " Why, sure—" Jack caught my idea, " you stick your fingers into a thick paste, and the finger is withdrawn coated with it. Ergo, your finger has touched nothing of what remains in the pot— or sack. Hooray for the Kid-Woman ! I salute ! "

After lunch we climbed a disgorged litter of boulders and sharp lava, to inspect the meagre crumbling ruins of fortifications built by Kamehameha the Great into the side of the mountain ;

then, overtopping the dizzy verge, we sank slowly into the ruddy depths, by way of the cinder declivities we had speculated upon from our lofty perch. Closer acquaintance proved them entirely too rough with loose rubble for tobogganing. The horses left sulphurous yellow tracks as they pulled their pasterns out of the bottomless burnt sands, and a golden streamer flew backward from each hoof-fall. So swift was our drop that riders strung out ahead speedily grew very, very small, though distinct, as if seen through the wrong end of a telescope. In the marvellously clear atmosphere each object stood out clean-cut ; while an insidious sunburn began to make itself felt on lips and cheeks and noses. Apart from slightly shortened breathing at the summit, we had felt no inconvenience from the elevation.

And so our caravan straggled into the deeps of Haleakala, sometimes a rider galloping springily across a dark cinder slope in a halo of tawny sun-shot dust, then dropping steeply, his horse nearly sitting ; while overhead and behind, on the evanescent trail of our making, came the picturesque packhorses and cowboys, and one small patient mule laden with camp comforts. From farthest below rose quaint reiterative chants of hulas, as Louis von Tempsky rode and sang, loose in the saddle, reins on his horse's neck, debonair and tireless, with a bonnie daughter to either side.

Strange is the furnishing of this stronghold

of the Sun God. And few are the spots in it that would invite the tired and thirsty wayfarer to tarry. For all the beauty of its rose and velvet of distance, there reigns intense desolation everywhere, with something sinister in the dearth of living plant or animal life. Passing an overhanging crimson Niagara of dead lava frozen in its fall, we reinvested the silent bleakness with old fire and flow and upheaval, until suddenly whooping into a mad race up the flanks of a big blow-hole that had earlier presented its dry throat to our downward gaze, we hesitated to look over into the noiseless pit, half-expecting we knew not what. No such luck, of course, although dead volcanoes have been known to come to life; and we slanted back into the floor of the House, and went on our burning, arid way.

It gives one an odd sensation to realize that one is traversing miles literally inside a high mountain. We thought of friends we should have liked to transport abruptly into the unguessable cavity. Strangely enough, as we progressed, it turned out that the warm colour, so vivid from the summit, flushes only one side of the cones, like a fever not burned out; although ahead, on the opposite wall, there is a giant scar of perfect rose.   .

At length we commenced to wind among little crateresque hillocks, clothed with rough growths by the healing hands of the millenniums, until, far on, we could just glimpse the Promised Rest of verdure—clustered trees and smiling pasture

where our tents were to be pitched for two nights[1]
while the beasts should graze.   But the distance
was as deceptive as a mirage, and we had still to
pick our way along many a sharp trail across fields
of clinking lava, black and fragile as jet, swirled
smoothly in the cooling and called *pahoehoe*;
while the *a-a* lava, twisted and tormented into
shapes of flame, licked against the sky above our
heads.   I never cease to feel a sense of aghastness
before these stiff, upstanding waves of the slow,
resistless molten rock, flung stark and frozen like
the still waters of the Red Sea of old ; and here,
amidst these carven surges are smooth sandy
levels, dotted with shrubs, where one may gallop
in and out as if on the floor of a recessant ocean.

Involved in a maze of wayward lava-flows
among little grey cones, the vast aspect of the
crater was lost, although, turning, we could yet
discern Magnetic Peak.   In every direction the
views changed from moment to moment ; and
wonder grew as we tried to grasp the immensity
of the old volcano and its astounding details.
Once we halted at the Bottomless Pit itself—
a blow-hole in the ground that had leisurely
spat liquid rock, flake upon flake, until around
its ugly mouth a wall accumulated, of material,
so glassy light that large pieces could easily
be broken off, and one must have a care not to
lean too heavily against it, for judged by the
soundless way the rock plummets were swallowed,
a human body falling into the well would never
be heard after its first cry.

There is but one chance to water animals until camp-ground is reached, and we found the pool dry—*auwe!* But the kanakas, carrying buckets, scaled the crater wall to a higher basin, from which they sent down a stream. One by one the horses drank while we rested in an oasis of long grass, cooling our flaming faces in the shade.

A mile or two more, and we reined up to the cracking of rifle-shots under the cliff at Paliku, a fairy nook of a camping spot, where Mr. Von and the cowboys, having beaten us in, were bringing down goat-meat for supper. I was guilty of inward treacherous glee that only one was hit, as that was plenty for our needs ; and the spotted kids looked so wonderful clambering a wall that apparently had no foothold.

Camp had been planned in a luxuriant grove of *opala* and *kolea* trees close to the foot of the pali ; but the ground was soggy from recent rains, and we found better tent-space in the open, where sleek cattle grazed not far off, getting both food and drink from the lush grass that grows the year round in this blossoming pocket of the desert. This reminds me that there are sections on the " dry " side of Maui where herds subsist entirely upon prickly cactus, having no other food or moisture. Only a few weaker ones succumb to the spines of the cactus, and it is said that there are no finer cattle on the islands than the survivors.

All took a hand in the task of settling camp,

we women filling interminable sacks with ferns, to serve as mattresses. The change of exercise was the best thing that could happen to us malihinis, else we might have suffered from the many hours in saddle.

And what a starved company it was that smacked its lips at smell of Von's jerked beef broiling on a stick over a fire at the open tent-flap,. behind which the rest of us sat and made ready the service on a blanket. For it is right chilly of an evening, nearly 7000 feet in the air —a veritable refrigerating plant in the mansion of the Sun.

I hope, if ever I land in heaven, and it is anything half as attractive as this earth I go marvelling through, that I shall not feel it incumbent upon me to keep a journal. Seeing and feeling are enough to keep one full occupied. And yet some one in my small family of two, it would seem, must chronicle the details of its colourful existence.

PALIKU, TO HANA, MAUI,
Thursday, July 18, 1907.

Too burned and tired to fancy goat-hunting in a steady rain, Mrs. Thurston and I spent yesterday resting, reading, sleeping, and playing cards in the dripping tent, while our men went with Mr. Von and the girls. The drenching clouds drifted and lifted on the pali where the sun darted golden javelins through showers until the raindrops broke into a glory of rainbows. Then the brief splendour waned, leaving us almost in darkness at midday, in an increasing downpour.

Our hunters returned in late afternoon, wet and weary, but jubilant and successful, eager for supper and a damp game of whist on the blankets. After we had tucked under those same blankets, with shrewdly placed cups to catch the leaks in our soaked tent-roof, we listened to the mellow voices of the Hawaiians singing little hulas and love-songs and laughing as musically.

This morning it was down-tent, and boots and saddles once more ; but ere we made our six o'clock get-away, I found a half-hour to go prowling to the foot of the pali, to an alluring spot that had been in my eye since the day before— a green lap in the grey rock where a waterfall had been. Winning through a nettly wet thicket, I peeped into a ferny, flowery corner of Elfland at the base of a vertical fall down which the water had furrowed a shining streak on the polished rock amid clinging, fanning ferns and grasses and velvet mosses—grotto fit for childhood's loveliest imaginings to people with pink and white fairy-folk and brown and green gnomes.

They were treacherous and slippery trails that led out of the crater and down through Kaupo Gap, chill with Naulu's draughty onslaught, where Pele, Goddess of Fire, broke through the wall of the crater and fled for ever from Maui to take up her abode on Mauna Loa's wounded side ; but soon we rode out of the clouds and went streaming in the horizontal rays of a glorious sunrise. Again we caught glimpses of Mauna Kea and Mauna Loa, supernal in the morning sky although a trifle more plausible seen from this lesser level.

Down our sure-footed animals dropped into lush meadows where fat cattle raised their heads to stare ; up and down across crackling lava beds, like wrecked giant stairways balustraded by the cool grey-and-gold walls of the Gap, from between which we could make out the surfy coast-line. Once we had struck the final descent, there were no ups, but only downs, for 6000 feet ; and several times our saddles, sliding over the necks of the horses, obliged us to dismount and set them back.

On a brown-rocky bluff above the sea we found an early lunch ready and waiting at the house of a Portuguese-Hawaiian family named Vieira, and by eleven were loping easily along green cliff, past old grass-houses still occupied by natives— a sight fast becoming rare. From one weirdly tattered hut, a nut-brown, wrinkled woman, old, but with fluffy black hair blown out from wild black eyes, rushed flinging her arms about and crying " Aloha ! Aloha ! " with peal upon peal of mad sweet laughter.

For several miles the coast was much like that of Northern California, with long points running out into the ocean ; but soon we were scrambling up and down gulch-trails. In olden times these

gulches were impassable on account of the tremendous rainfall on this eastern shore, averaging
200 inches yearly. (Three years ago it registered
as high as 420 inches.) So the wise chiefs, somewhere around the sixteenth century, with numerous commoners at their command, had the curt
zigzags paved with a sort of cobble-stone, without regard to ease of grade, and the rises and falls
of this slippery highway are nothing short of
formidable, especially when one's horse,
accustomed to leading, resents being curbed
midway of the procession and repeatedly tries
to rush past the file where there is no passing-
room.

But the animals quickly proved that they
could take perfect care of themselves and their
riders, and we advantaged by the welcome assurance to look our fill upon the beautiful coast
and forested mountain. Tiny white beaches
dreamed in the sunlight at the feet of the gulch-
valleys, where rivers flowed past coco-nut palms
that leaned and swayed in the strong sea-breeze,
and brown babies tumbled among tawny grass-
huts, and gay calicoes, hung out to dry, furnished
just the right note of brilliant colour.

Some of the idyllic strands were uninhabited
and inviting ; and we spoke of the tired dwellers
of the cities of all the world who never heard of
Windward Maui, where is space, and solitude, and
beauty, warm winds and cool, soothing rainfalls,
fruit and flowers for the plucking, swimming by
seashore and hunting on mountain-side, and

Mauna Kea over there a little way to gladden eye and spirit. Then, " Mate, are you glad you're alive ? " broke upon my reverie, as Jack leaned from his horse on a zigzag above my head.

It would not have seemed like Hawaii if we had not traversed a cane planation, and halt was made at the Kipahulu Sugar Mill, while Gwen's horse must have a shoe reset. It would appear that the onyx feet of the unshod horses, that have never worn iron in their lives, stand the wear and tear of the incalculably hard travel over the ripping lava better than the more pampered animals.

All the eager train knew from happy experience that at Hana waited their fodder ; and we, their riders, in like frame of mind, restrained them not. We had done thirty-five miles when we pulled up before the small hotel—and such miles ! Mr, Cooper, Manager of Hana Plantation, called upon us with extra delicacies to eke out the plain hotel fare—avocados, luscious papaias, and little sugary bananas. " Gee ! " murmured Jack, from the buttery depths of a big alligator pear " I wish we could grow these things in the Valley of the Moon ! "

This village of Hana lies high on the horseshoe of a little blue bay embraced by two headlands, and is fraught with warlike legend and history. In the eighteenth century, King Kalaniopuu, of the old dynasty, whose life was one long bloody battle with other chiefs of Maui for the possession of these eastern districts, held the

southern headland of the bay, Kauiki, for over
twenty years ; then the great Kahekili deprived
the garrison of its water-supply, and retook the
fort, which is an ancient crater. In the time of
Kamehameha, this fort withstood his attacks
for two years, after the remainder of Maui had
been brought to his charmed heel.

To-night, I know, I shall fall unconscious with,
in my ears, the ringing of iron hoofs on stony
pathways, and the gurgle and plash of waterfalls.

HANA, TO KEANAE VALLEY, MAUI,
Saturday, July 20, 1907.

The Ditch Country—this is the unpoetical,
unimaginative name of a wonderland that eludes
description. An island world in itself, it is
compounded of vision upon vision of heights
and depths, hung with waterfalls, withal of a
gentle grandeur, clothed softly with greenest
green of tree and shrub and grass, ferns of endless
variety, fruiting guavas, bananas, mountain-
apples—all in a warm, glowing, tropical tangle ;
a Land of Promise for generations to come, for
all who can sit a Haleakala horse—the best
mountain horse on earth—must come some day
to feast their eyes upon this possession of the
United States whose beauty, we are assured of
the surprising fact, is unknown except to perhaps
100 white men. This of course is exclusive of
the engineers of the trail and ditch and those
financially interested in the plantations of Wind-

ward Maui. And undoubtedly no white foot ever previously trod here.

The Ditch Country—an untrammelled paradise wherein an intrepid engineer yclept O'Shaughnessy overcame formidable odds and put through a magnificent irrigation scheme that harnessed the abundant waterfalls and tremendously increased the output of the invaluable sugar planations And to most intents it remains an untrammelled paradise, for what little the traveller glimpses of the fine achievement of the Nahiku Ditch itself is in the form of a wide concrete waterway running for short infrequent distances beside the grassy trail before losing itself in Mr. O'Shaughnessy's difficult tunnels through which most of its course is quarried.

All manner of Hawaiian timber goes to make up the imcomparable foresting of this great mountain-side whose top is lost in the clouds. Huge koa trees, standing or fallen, the dead swathed in vines, the quick embraced by the *ie-ie*, a climbing palm that clings only to living pillars, its blossoming arms hanging in curves like cathedral candelabra ; the *ohia ai*, lighting the prevailing green with its soft thistle-formed crimson brushed and cherry-red fruit ; the *ohia lehua*, prized for its splendid dark brown hardwood, but bearing no edible fruit ; and the kukui, silver-green as young chestnuts in spring-time, trooping up hill and down dale. Especially ornamental are the luxuriant tree-ferns on their chocolate-brown hairy pedestals, and many of the ground-ferns were familiar—even the gold and silver-back grow in Hawaii, Indeed a fern-collector would be in his element in these islands. Maui alone has all of 130 odd varieties.

We nooned on a rubber plantation in which Mr. Thurston is financially interested. Indeed, we have yet to learn of any Hawaii enterprise of importance in which he is not, including, which we have but lately learned, the Haleakala Ranch, in which he, James B. Castle, and H. B. Baldwin each own one-third. Mr. and Mrs Anderson entertained us at a hospitable luncheon, served by two kimono'd Japanese maids—little bits of pictures off a fan, Jack observed. He, by the way, well nigh disgraced himself when, replying to a query from his hostess whether or not he liked foreign dishes, he assured her he enjoyed all good foods of all countries, with one exception —" nervous" pudding, which he declared made him tremble internally. The words and accompanying gestures were still in the air when' a maid entered bearing the dessert—a trembling watermelon-hued dome of gelatine ! A horrified silence was broken by Mr. Anderson's shout of laughter, in which every one joined with relief. But Jack consistently declined any part of the " nervous " confection, saying that he always preferred coffee alone for his dessert.

Armine, to the surprise of her father and sister, and my speechless delight, offered to let me ride her superb Bedouin for the afternoon, a young horse with gait so springy that he seemed treading

in desert sand.   We had travelled nearly all day in
heavy showers, and were convinced of the accur-
acy of the figures of Woodward Maui's annual
rainfall, for no saddle-slicker was able to exclude
the searching sky-shot water.   But the discomfort of wet-clinging garments was lost in our rapt
attention to the increasing marvel of the landscape.   Rightly did our guides assure us that
yesterday's scenery was as nothing compared
to this, where the waterfalls ever increased in
height and volume, thundering above and sometimes clear over the trail quarried into a wall of
rock that extended thousands of feet over our heads
and a thousand sheer below the narrow foothold.   Our brains swam with the whirling,
shouting wonder of waters, the yawning depths
that opened below our feet, filled with froth of wild
new rivers born of the fresh rains.   Jack's warning
was true : I have saved no words for this final
stunning spectacle.

We reached Keanae Valley tired in body, in
eye, in mind—aye, even surfeited with beauty.
But once in dry clothing weariness fell from us,
as we disposed ourselves in reclining rattan
chairs on a high porch of the little house, and leisurely counted the cataracts fringing the valley
amphitheatre, upon whose turrets the sunset
sky, heavy with purple and rose and gold, seemed
to rest.   Altogether we made out thirty-five,
some of them dropping hundreds of feet, making
hum the machinery in great sugar mills elsewhere.
Commercialism in grand Keanae !   And yet, it

is not out of the way of romance to associate the
idea of these tremendous natural forces with
the mighty enginery that man's thinking machinery
has evolved for them to propel in the performance of his work.

KEANAE VALLEY, TO HALEAKALA RANCH,
Sunday, July 21, 1907.

Mr. Von had us stirring by half-past six, after
ten hours in bed. So soundly had we been sunk
in " the little death in life," that even a violenty
driven rain which thoroughly soaked our dried
riding togs, hanging on chairs in the middle of
the room, failed to disturb. We experienced
the novel sensation of shivering in a tropic vale,
the while pulling on water-logged corduroy and
khaki, even hats being soggy.

After a breakfast of wild bananas, boiled taro,
poi, broiled jerked beef and fresh milk, we fared
forth out of the wondrous mist-wreathed valley
and up-trail on horses spurred with knowledge of
this last stretch to home stables. The air was
ineffably clear, as if from a cleansing bath, with
only light clouds in the sunny sky to rest the
eyes.

More ditch trails and jungle of unwithering
green, sparkling wet, and steaming rainbows
in the slanting sungold of the morning ; more
and still more wonderful gulches, to make good
Mr. Von's overnight prophecy. And we traversed
a succession of make-shift bridges that called
for the best caution of the horses who knew the

every unstable inch. Jack, pacing behind on
the many-gaited Pontius Pilate, told me afterward that his heart was in his throat to see the
slender spans give to the weight and swinging
motion of my stout charger, who, still fretting
at being withheld from the lead, pranced scandal-
ously in the most unwise places.

At length we approached a promised " worst
and last gulch," a flood-eroded, lofty ravine of
appalling beauty, down the pitch of which we slid
with bated breath, to the reverberation of great
falls on every hand. Obeying Mr. Von's serious
behest, we gathered on the verge of a roaring
torrent over-flung by a mere excuse for a bridge,
not more than four feet wide, roughly fifty feet
long, and innocent of railing. To our left the
main cataract sprayed us in its pounding fall to
a step in the rocky defile where it crashed just
under the silly bridge, thence bursting out in
deafening thunder to its mightiest plunge,
immediately below, cascading to the sea.

" Now, hurry and tell Von what you want,"
Jack shouted in my ear above the watery din.
And what I wanted was to be allowed to precede
the others over this bridge—oh, not in bravado,
believe—quite the contrary. I was in a small
terror of the thing, but, since it had to be crossed,
I was determined if possible to cross it by the
least risky method. Fact was, I feared to trust
the Welchman, justly intolerant of his enforced
degradation to the ranks, not to make a headlong
rush to overtake his rival, Mr. Von's horse, should

he lead, for a single rider at a time was to be permitted on the swaying structure.

Without discussion, Mr. Von appreciated and consented; and when the order of march was arranged, the Welchman proved his right to leadership without hesitation, wise muzzle between his exact feet, sniffing, feeling, every narrow plank of the unsteady way. It was an experience big with thought—carrying with it an intense sense of aloneness, aloofness from aid in event of disaster, trusting the vaunted human of me without reserve to the instinct and intelligence of a "lesser animal." The blessed Welchman!— with chaos all about and little foundation for security, trembling but courageous, he won slowly step by step across the roaring white destruction and struck his small fine hoofs into firm rising ground once more.

With brave set face Harriet Thurston came next after Mr. Von, and her ambitious but foolhardy steed, midway of the passage, began jogging with eagerness to be at the end, setting up a swaying rhythm of the bridge that sent sick chills over the onlookers, and it was with immense relief we watched him gain solid earth. Pontius Pilate bore Jack sedately across, followed by the little girls.

It may give some faint conception of the scariness of this adventure, to tell an incident related by Mr. Von. One of his cowboys, noted on Maui for his fearlessness, always first in the pen with a savage bull, and first on the wildest bucking bronco off range, absolutely balked at riding this final test of all our nerve : " I have a wife and family," he expostulated ; then dismounted and led his horse across.[1]

KALEINALU, MAUI,
Tuesday, July 23, 1907

Kaleinalu, " Wreath of Billows," the seaside retreat of the von Tempskys, is but another illustration of the ideal chain of conditions that marks existence in these fabulous isles. Jack is almost incoherent on the subject of choice of climates and scenery and modes of living to be found from mountain-top to shore. One may sleep comfortably under blankets at Ukulele and Paliku, with all the invigoration of the temperate zone ; enjoy mild variable weather at 4000 feet, as at the Ranch ; or lie at warm sea-level, under a sheet or none, blown over by the flowing trade-wind. " Watch out, Mate," he warns me ; " I'm likely to come back here to live some day, when we have gone round the world and back— if I don't get too attached to the Valley of the Moon." And he ceases not to marvel that the shore-line is not thronged with globe trotters bickering for beach lots. It is a wonderful watering place for old and young, with finest of sand for the babies to play in, and exciting surfing inside protecting reef for swimmers.

---

[1] Ours was the last party that ever crossed this bridge. A new one was hung shortly afterward.

And here we malahinis are resting, after one day of tennis and colt-breaking up-mountain, from our six days in the saddle. Nothing more arduous fills the hours than swinging in hammocks over the sand in a shady ell of the beach-house, reading, playing whist, swimming in water more exhilarating than at Waikiki, romping, sleeping —and eating, fingering our poi and kukui-nut and lomi'd salmon with the best.

To-morrow we bid good-bye to these new, fine friends, who must have sensed our heart of love for them and their wonderland, for they beg us to return, ever welcome, to their unparalleled hospitality. By now we have proudly come into our unexpected own, with a translation of our name into the Hawaiian tongue, worked out by Kakina and Mr. Von, who speak like natives with the natives, and sometimes with each other, while the speech of the lassies abounds in the pretty colloquialisms of their birthland.

Always they say *pau* for connotation of " finish," or " that will do " or " enough " ; *kokua* for help; noun or verb—or, in the sense of approval, or permission ; *hapai* is to carry ; *hiki no*, as we should say " all right," " very well," ; *hele mai* or *pimai*, come here, or go there ; one oftenest hears *pilikia* for trouble, difficulty, or *aole pilikia* for the harmonious negative ; the classic *awiwi*, hurry, has been superseded by that expressive and sharply explosive slang, *wikiwiki ;* and when this loveliest of hostesses orders a bath prepared, she enunciates *auau* to the Japanese maids.

Most commands, however, are given in mixed English-Hawaiian. The old pure word for food, and to eat, *paina*, is never heard, for the Chinese kowkow—*kaukau* in the Hawaiian adaptation —has likewise come to stay.

Von's most peremptory commands often trail into the engaging *eh?* that charmed our ears the first day at Pearl Lochs. And so, as I say, upon us has been bestowed the crowning grace of all the gracious treatment accorded upon Maui—the Hawaiian rendering of London, which is *Lakana ;* although how London can be transmuted into Lakana is as much a mystery as the mutation of Thurston into Kakina. At any rate, my pleased partner struts as Lakana Kanaka (kanaka means literally *man*), while meekly I respond to Lakana Wahine.

For the continuation of Mr. and Mrs. Jack London's travels see "Jack London in the Southern Seas."

Printed in Great Britain by Butler & Tanner, Frome and London

www.ingramcontent.com/pod-product-compliance
Lightning Source LLC
LaVergne TN
LVHW011346080426
835511LV00005B/141